SIMPLY
PAY
ATTENTION

Peter A. Luber

Sageous
New York
2011

Sageous
Amsterdam, NY 12010

First published in 2011
By Sageous

Simply Pay Attention / Peter A. Luber
ISBN: 978-0-615-45417-7

CONTENTS

Introduction...7

Brief History...13

The Seven Souls.....................................23

The Prophet...33

First Dream Encounter: Ashley..............45

Thought Energy.....................................51

First Dream Encounter: Ted.................57

Attention...61

First Dream Encounter: Louis.............67

Awareness...71

First Dream Encounter: Howard...........75

Lucid Dreaming....................................79

First Dream Encounter: The Interview....93

The Charge..103

First Dream Encounter: Gloria............109

The Future..113

Introduction

First, there is no God.

Okay. That is not entirely true. There *was* a God, or rather a being who invented our reality, creating with one thought all that we know. This being did exist, once, and it did so in a state of perfection unfettered by things like time or space -- that existence was enjoyed, by it and seven other equally perfect entities, *before* it created the universe; what happened to their existence after the Big Bang is partially what this book is about. Instead of calling that being "God," a term heavily burdened with religious and mythological baggage, this book will apply the slightly less lofty moniker of "Soul" to this being, and its seven siblings. The reasoning behind this name will be clarified as well.

When this Soul created the universe -- on a whim, apparently -- it deleted itself in the process. The remaining Seven Souls are either unwilling or unable to explain why this self-erasure occurred. What we do know is that in place for the Eighth Soul's existence were left this universe, our physical time/space continuum, and a real problem for those remaining Seven Souls.

The Souls are and always were comprised of a unique energy that will be referred to as "thought energy," or occasionally just "thought." Thought energy is exactly what it sounds like: the energy created by the processing of a conscious thought. Though it may sound a bit counter-intuitive, thought energy preceded the existence of our physical universe. Once, before the term itself could exist, thought was all there was; no more, no less. This thought energy was being created by the conscious activity of the eight original Souls. And that was all there was -- no time, no space; just eight Souls existing as sentient entities in quiet perfection.

So, before the Big Bang, some eight distinct beings existed, purely and of only themselves. Their presence was perfect, their thought energy eternal and uncorrupted by time, space, or emotion. Then one of the Eight, feeling a need for more, instigated the Big Bang. Its action converted the consciousnesses of the remaining seven into matter and energy. This conversion forced the Seven Souls to be dispersed throughout the new physical universe -- still a part of everything, but weakened, and imprisoned by a new perfection beyond their power: the laws of physics. From that eighth Soul's work came the universe, the dissolution of the Souls, sentient physical life, and ultimately, as we speak, us. On top of all of that, and to underline a major purpose of this book, we, the human race, may very well be uniquely qualified to undo the mistake that started it all, to free the Souls. This is an opportunity that could change the face of human existence.

Now to what this book is about:

- Energy. This book is about energy. We have heard much from many that everything is, in the end, energy. That is true and, as such, energy itself is better described in other oft substantial tomes written by folks with proper training in math and physics. Suffice it to say here that, aside from gravity, the energy in the textbooks is that which was proscribed by the Eighth Soul before the Big Bang to follow the set of specific rules needed to hold a universe together. That is well and good, and every observer should mind the physicists' posits. Yet, aside from what has been discovered, described, and almost religiously adhered to, a major factor of our reality has been omitted by the modern cosmos modelers. There is another energy that this book will seek to discuss at some length: that energy is that which is created by the action of conscious thought. Every time you have a thought, make a decision, build a sentence, or even admire a sunset, you are generating thought energy. Do not confuse thought energy with the electromagnetic energy the brain produces as a result of processing perceptions, physical expressions, memories, etc. Those are well documented already and metaphysically inconsequential. No; the thought energy this book will discuss is the actual energy *created* every time a new thought enters physical reality. This energy does not exist in any of the mathematical models of the universe. In a sense, it runs anathema to the rules created by the Big Bang. It defies Newton in that its energy did not exist before the thought that made it was conceived – there is no conversion here, no conservation. Only creation. Thought energy is unique. It fails to fall nicely into the theories of everything, and by all physical rules should not exist. And yet it does. Because the physical world does not have a mathematical formula on hand to describe or quantify thought energy, it resides just outside of humanity's version of reality. Because it exists outside our reality does not mean that thought energy does not exist, however, or that it cannot influence our reality and change our lives.

• This book is partially about the original progenitors of all thought energy. They existed before space and time, they permeate all reality to this day, and they form the basis of all human potential. These are the Seven Souls, the beings who shared an existence with an Eighth Soul until it desired more. These Seven have been waiting for billions of years for a sentient species to assist them in renewing their original perfectly time and space exempt existence.

• These Souls have found a species that can help them: humanity, and now they have also found a human avatar to present their message to the rest of humanity, at least those who will listen, through their dreams. How does he do it? Why does he do it? Who is he? What does he want us to do? Those questions and others will be addressed.

• This book is about self-awareness, the single physical act that sets humanity apart from almost every other species on earth (or anywhere else, for that matter). Everything – thought energy, the plight of the Seven Souls, the adventures of their messenger, the potential transcendental experience of those humans who heed the messenger, indeed the ability to grasp these concepts and all others which have yet to be exposed to us – is centered upon self-awareness. Self-awareness is the lynch-pin of the Souls' plan to bring us on board their cosmic ship – without it we cannot participate at all, much less transcend to a state of being compatible with that of the Souls, and capable of sharing their joy, their adventure, their being. On a more practical bent, self-awareness is also the foundation for lucid dreaming, which is the only tool the Souls and their avatar have found to successfully forge that first step in the long path toward uniting with them and freeing us all.

• This book is about paying attention.

It may sound like a simple thing, but in truth it is the attribute in which humanity as a race is most lacking. Attention may have become such an evolutionary no-brainer that even thinking people have come to take it for granted. This is a mistake: attention is critical for self-awareness, for learning, for communication, and for opening the very large heavily bolted gates that lie between the Souls and us. The ability to pay attention, and to develop self-awareness, will change everything for all humanity. We simply must do it. Unfortunately, this book is not about how to pay attention – that skill is up to every individual to master (or simply recall from their most primitive roots). It does attempt to point out why it is so important to revitalize this forgotten skill. Though on paper its mastery is quite simple, in reality paying attention might be the most difficult skill any sentient being can develop.

• This book, finally, is about a call to transcendence. That call comes to us from the Souls, and, though they do so for their rescue alone, the byproduct of returning the Souls to their natural state may well be the next step in human evolution. Both the knowledge humans pick up from communicating directly with the Souls and the opportunity to "fill the gap" they will leave when they exit our reality may present opportunities for spiritual and physical growth that have never been available to another species. Ever. And the few who are on the crest of the wave of human ascension in the wake of the Souls' redemption will reap the greatest rewards, the most profound of which might just be the psychic wherewithal to survive the coming inevitable changes to what it means to be human; and those changes will be too substantial and abrupt to be survived with the tools given us by nature.

Since that redemption will likely take many, many years, those riding that crest will enjoy the ability to explore, through the Souls, the secrets of a dynamic universe and the joy inherent in the experience of forms of communication and enlightenment beyond anything our current philosophies can imagine. The possibilities the Souls present are nearly limitless, and any person can encounter them simply by paying attention, and by caring about the rest of their race.

This book is *not* a scientific study, and in no way dares to be scholarly, empirical, or even terribly rational. It may offer up a few twists on our current remarkably raw understanding of reality, as well as humanity's place in it all, but it does not seek to prove anything. Proofs are boring, rarely believed, and, when discussing the metaphysical, prone to being interpreted by "experts" as incorrect.

Finally, this book is not a theological treatise. On the contrary, the contents of this book do not require a leap, or even small step, of faith to be believed. The reality of what is professed in these pages can be proven (or disproved, as it were) by you the reader, provided you are focused, disciplined, very imaginative, learn to lucid dream, and, of course, pay attention. So, the things discussed in this book are real or they are not -- that is for you to discover, on your own.

A Brief History

Before the beginning there was nothing. Before our 'everything' came to be, there existed no time, no space, no weak forces, strong forces, or Higgs bosons. There was nothing at all. Nothing that we could name, were we there. But the cosmos, though devoid of our stuff, was occupied, even before there was anything. It was occupied by thought energy.

This thought energy was aware, focused, and conscious in an eightfold manner. Eight loci of sentience, the Primordial Souls, shared an existence bathed in perfection, peace, and grace, utterly unfettered by physical reality. They knew of each other, and communicated in their own fashion, but with no universe or dimensions of space and time to clutter their perfectly shared existence, they felt no need to chat. Perhaps they should have.

Somehow, one Soul defied its nature and became restless. It grew aware that simple perfection would not do; it desired creation. It desired, period. It considered the singularity that was the Eight's universe, and sensed potential. What the potential was, it could not know, but it did sense how to release it. So it did.

With that single thought our universe was born. The Eight Souls' world was transformed into fuel for the Big

Bang. The energy released by the subsequent formation of our universe sprayed the Souls' essences evenly and thinly throughout the entirety of what we now call time and space. Perfection, vaporized by the will of one errant Soul, was a memory the other Seven could but endure for the palpable eternity that they now experienced as the passage of time. Their awareness grew weak as the Souls' essence raced outward, obliged as it was by the new laws created by the errant Eighth that required it to occupy every new atom that would ever exist. That occupation was benign, however, because the Souls' awareness, their existence, their nature, was still thought. Thought survived the big bang as the one form of energy that had not been included in the laws of physics as set by the errant Soul. So not only did the Seven have their essence diffused into every atom of the universe, but their only source of power, thought, had no effect on the Eighth's creation. The Seven have thus been helpless, endlessly waning, and eternally attached to a universe not of their making, all the while fully conscious of their plight, and their past.

Of that Eighth Soul, nothing remains. Though it was the creator of our universe, and everything in all existence can be traced back to its single instantaneous whim, its flash of desire for something new proved to be a curse. As best as can be understood, that something new it created engulfed the errant Soul's consciousness, masking its awareness in a skein of joy for its new creation. Its essence was lost to the cosmos, barely a morsel of memory for the remaining and struggling Seven Souls, long before its creation cast its first glimmer of light.

For the Seven, that first 300,000 years spent in darkness were the most difficult. They had not known darkness -- or light -- before the Big Bang, and its existence deeply disturbed them. Nature, their empty yet all-powerful new master, threatened to crush them in darkness before anything at all existed, save time. But the Seven persevered, witnessed the first burst of light, then the birth of stars, galaxies, planets, and life.

In a sense, the Souls are responsible for the organized universe. The "rules," as written by the errant Soul, contained three forces: electromagnetism, and the weak and strong atomic forces. There was initially no gravity. It turns out that as the Souls communicated, both with themselves as they spread across the cosmos and with each other, they created an intricate, fantastically organized, and permanent pattern of pathways on which their thought energy traveled. These paths formed a structural basis for the matter and energy produced by the Big Bang, that basis being gravity.

The creation of gravity, and thus the forming of galaxies, planets, and life, ultimately led to sentient life. Because sentient life creates organized thought energy (more on that later) it is uniquely connected to both nature and the Souls. It holds in its natural ability to create thought energy an innate advantage to manipulate realty that the Souls simply do not possess. So, as sentient beings, we are currently the Souls' latest best opportunity to return to a state of eternal perfection. That said, there is a chance that the Souls may have recognized the value of cosmic organization toward returning to their original state and actually planned gravity, and its fruits, all along. They are not telling.

As the universe progressed, the Souls became a vague, detached audience, and their interest grew weaker as the universe suffered them to expand ever further from that original singularity. After many billions of years of dissolution in the growing physical universe, they knew they were likely doomed to a permanent, potentially meaningless existence among the relentless rules of the errant Eighth's hapless creation. The only hope to which they could cling was that the universe would eventually collapse into itself, restoring their primordial existence. That was a distant hope, however, and clinging to it was poor exercise for their dwindling awareness. They also became cognizant of the fact that even if the universe did collapse back into a singularity, that would happen long after their consciousness had been spread so thinly that they would lack the mental cohesion needed to regain their original selves, or anything similar.

In time a new opportunity for the Souls to restore their original state emerged. The Souls learned after uncounted millennia that the driver of their awareness, thought, had come into existence in many living beings throughout their unwanted universe. They had been observing life take form from its beginnings, but initially found little value in it beyond a time-killing curiosity. Now life offered them their first surprise since the Big Bang. As it evolved into more complex forms, some of these forms began to hint at a new window for salvation for the Seven: Beings other than themselves were thinking. Sentience, and its commensurate thought energy, was at hand.

The Seven knew immediately what needed to be done. Since the foundation of their existence was thought, and since their essence permeated all things, they concluded that it would be only a matter of time before they could make their existence known to these new sentient organic beings. To the Souls it seemed simple enough: since the universe itself breathed their existence, they couldn't help but be discovered among the thoughts of these new, thinking organic beings. Once they were discovered, there may be a chance for communication. Should communication be achieved, these living organic beings might manage to incorporate the Souls into this new reality, this physical universe, in a manner that would allow their awareness to gather meaningfully into itself, and both avoid ultimate dissolution while also letting the Eighth's physical creation continue unscathed.

So the Souls began to watch for thinking beings. They learned to prepare to respond coherently, should one sentient being come to cast its awareness upon them. That was not easy, and the wait was far longer than anticipated, because the Seven had not accounted for imagination. The Souls, who lack imagination themselves, did not anticipate that their act of contacting sentient physical beings would inspire those beings to interpret the encounter, rather than take it at face value. For many millennia, the young beings would create a new religion or mythology to explain each new encounter with the Seven, regularly setting the Souls back many generations as dogma displaced the possibility of understanding by the group from which whatever being they contacted represented. The Seven realized in time that they needed more than sentience to communicate. The beings must develop and maintain a certain spiritual maturity that would allow them to pay attention long enough to enable conversation.

Even before that, on earth that maturity nearly surfaced once, with a race of dinosaurs we know as velociraptors (they called themselves, phonetically, the KKalklem, but we will stay with the more familiar 'raptors,' since none are left to complain). The raptors successfully dominated the earth in a most productive manner for millennia, and some had actually listened when they encountered the Souls during quiet contemplation. Sadly for the Souls, however, the raptors allowed the concrete reassurance of technology to undermine their spiritual existence during the centuries they spent preparing to escape earth before the Great Comet hit (they did, by the way). Though some raptors had heard and understood the Souls, it did not matter: they had forsaken such spiritual growth in the name of survival, and all their attention went to building star-spanning transportation for their people.

Successful connection was also achieved much later at separate times with the cetaceans and ant colonies. Both of those races, though they understood the Souls' message and were spiritually advanced enough to pay attention, chose not to help the Souls restore themselves, for fear that such a change might end the near perfect spiritual existence they had already established for themselves through thoughtful evolution. The Souls understood. What else could they do? They sighed, as it were, and continued to wait. In a very short time, from their perspective, they noticed the development of a new being: Humans.

The dwindling Souls held out much hope for a new race on earth that eventually called themselves humans. Human thought energy was in particularly fine tune with that of the Souls. Initially this fact frustrated the Souls: for millennia billions of humans bathed them in thought energy, but the new sentients would not be spoken to, and it wasn't by choice. The usual nonsense followed every early encounter: religions, superstition, often war and great societal pain. Human imagination was so intense that contact with the Souls was actually a dangerous long-term event, in almost every case. The Seven were patient, however, and very old already. They sensed something special in this new race, and chose to wait for them. In time, the Souls were rewarded.

During the twentieth century, the Seven noticed that some humans were taking their dreams more seriously – not as symbolic messages, or as supernatural adventures; humans had been wasting their time in those endeavors for millennia. No, they were considering their dreams an extension of their consciousness, a new vehicle for self-exploration. A few were even trying to bring their sentient self-awareness into their dreams with them, in the form of lucid dreaming. The Seven saw that the door was open. They stepped through.

For almost a century, lucid dreamers were as frustrating a lot as any other groups the Souls had tried to work with in the past. Though they managed to carry their awareness through to their world of dreams, human lucid dreamers usually refused to release their imaginations, and for quite some time invariably incorporated the Souls' shouts into their dream images as some misunderstood self-styled metaphor, thus missing the call, and, worse, lending yet more mythology to the experience. The Souls were at an impasse: humans needed metaphor to understand their reality, but needed to transcend metaphor (or at least set it aside) to understand the Souls. What the Souls ultimately sought was a human dreamer who abandoned metaphor during his lucid dreams and welcomed experience beyond his ability to understand – the Souls knew they could work with that. In time, about midway through the twentieth century, they found one. He was a young man from somewhere in North America. The Seven began to communicate with this prospect.

They did so by initially presenting themselves in symbols and images the human could understand, careful to steer him away from archetypes that would distract him. Over the course of many lucid encounters, the dreamer learned to understand the Souls and their cause. He did not fear the change a resuscitation of the Seven might bring, but rather welcomed it as the next step in his own, and humanity's, evolution. The Seven did not agree, but allowed his hopes to endure, thus nurturing their communication.

The Seven taught the man to merge his consciousness with theirs, to work with thought energy in a manner that brought him into direct contact with all things -- in other words, the essence of the Souls. Needless to say that was a bit much for the man, so the Souls led him toward direct contact only with his own race. He became their avatar to humanity, able to communicate with any human during their dreams. Now, the Seven had been able to do this at any time throughout the existence of sentient life, but their calls, though occasionally heard (more later), were never properly attended. The Souls believed that this human avatar would bridge the gap between their pure – albeit very weak – thought and human thought. The man could teach his people to grow their awareness, to form their thoughts in a manner that might focus vast sums of thought energy to a new single locus into which the Souls could merge, and return to their previous, perfect existence.

And so, the Seven Souls sent their avatar forth into the dreams of men, assigning that avatar a single task: teach humanity to pay attention.

The avatar, or prophet, as his attentive hosts tend to call him, initially did not fully understand the depth of his assignment. Nevertheless, he dove into the dreams of his fellow humans and struggled to bring them into the fold of awareness, of true growth toward something beyond simple human experience: something truly eternal. He suffered much failure in his first journeys into the tattered psyches of his dreaming brethren, but he learned, with some subtle help from the Souls, how to listen for dreamers who might be open to his visit, who might welcome him and his message into their ethereal worlds. What that message was, the man himself was initially not quite sure, and upon waking he rarely remembered his adventures as little more than dreams that 'must have meant something.'

With such little instruction, the prophet chose simply to quietly insist that receptive dreamers remember themselves in all things they did and, above all, to remember that the most basic rule of human life was to be nice to others, and allow them to be nice to you. His quiet insistence goes almost universally unheeded, though, since the prophet visits dreamers as symbols or images that the *dreamers* created, thus he might appear in a dream as a stranger, an old friend, or even an inanimate object, and it is up to the dreamer to recognize him and then both hear and heed his message. Heeding the message of, say, an umbrella stand in the corner of a dreamscape is something even the most enlightened dreamer might have trouble doing. With that tiny repertoire, the prophet traveled for many decades among the dreams of humans; teaching, helping, and, above all, waiting with open arms. In time he mastered the ability to listen, subtly contribute, and softly advise from the outskirts of lucid dreamers' minds. He waited for them to notice him, or at least the idea that he represented. When they did, he sought to teach them to understand that there is more to reality than their sciences and religions teach. He reminds dreamers that their soul is not a possession but a thought-energy manifestation of their own consciousness; ultimately an eternal version of them that it is fully capable of true perfection without the aid of petty dogma or artificial sacrifice. Some listened, and woke feeling strangely content in the morning, the usual weight of a new day lifted, replaced by the joy of self-awareness and a night well spent. Others noted but fought the prophet's presence, denied the chance of his existence, and certainly never felt the prophet's message. Yet they know he was there, *in* their dreams yet not *of* their dreams. Though these were the great majority of sleeping minds the prophet visited, the Souls instructed him to let them past: humanity was at the cusp of awareness, certainly not engulfed in it. So, absent a leap in psychic evolution, those who chose not to listen were best left alone, and behind. This saddened the prophet, but he understood, and pressed on until he had gained the attention of enough sleeping minds that his presence became an archetype rather than an aberration. Then travel became easier, though the prophet still did not fully understand his purpose.

Which brings us to this day. The prophet strives to be present in the lucid dreams of attentive humans, and patiently waits for those dreamers to pay attention to him. Once they do, he kindles in them a hope that there is a meaning in their existence that transcends daily life and the erroneously based tenets of current religions. But because the Seven cannot or will not communicate this value, the attentive humans must take it on faith that their efforts are for the good, and not meant to hasten entropy. They rely on the pure good will of the prophet to bolster their faith, and to eventually further enlighten them to the goodness of their end.

The Seven Souls

Though 'Soul' is not an accurate label to apply to the Seven, and its use may cause more confusion than clarity, the prophet insists that it is the best term available. Though the word 'soul' in human nomenclature ultimately identifies nothing, the word itself carries value because it gently plucks a chord that resonates deeply in the psyche of most of us. 'Soul' is indeed one of the few words in any language that cannot be used in a negative manner. This is not an accident.

It is a given at this point that the Seven Souls no longer occupy a singularity absent any hint of time and space. It is also a given that they are now thinly dispersed throughout the universe their sibling created, with their essence diffused among every atom in the cosmos. However, do not let those givens lead you to conclude that the Seven were completely shorn of their individual identities as they dissipated, or that the thought energy that composes each of them diminished. Instead, try to understand that their consciousness is now, in a word, everywhere. Though their dispersion has left them weak, unable to do much more than observe the universe that imprisons them, the Souls are definitely still conscious, still sentient, and still very much aware.

Existing anywhere and everywhere in the entire universe might not sound like much of a prison to us but for the Souls, it is. Sure, they are everywhere, but their thoughts move without authority in our universe, not for lack of power but for lack of association. Their perfection is based upon an energy that would have little to do with the created universe, so by our measure they are physically quite weak. However, their minds draw from experience encompassing billions of years in our universe alone, let alone their eternal existence pre Big Bang. Though fully immersed in our universe, they simply do not belong to it. Their will does not function well in the structured world their brother created. They do know exactly how to leave it (without, the prophet assures, erasing the existing new life – like us), but they lack the power to do so.

Humans are strong. Their brains, having evolved from the base of the physical universe, are naturally integral to the energy that permeates (and allows for) everything we know as real. Human evolution also developed a trait that has slightly separated humanity from the rest of nature: sentience. Since humans can be self-aware, they have a rare gift: individual humans produce, through the generation of sentient thought, the same energy that would embody the Souls, should they ever regain cohesion. Human thought, therefore, is key to the souls' salvation. When the Souls sensed the earliest presence of human thought energy at its inception millions of years ago, they began their vigil. They understood that their long wait might come to nothing, as had happened many times in the past. This was because, aside from the very rare exception, even the most thoughtful beings failed to notice that their mental activity was the source for an energy type that cannot, by rule of physics, exist in nature. By that same inconsistency, thought could cause the souls to regain their existence. They understood, and took an interest in us; especially those rare exceptions. And they waited.

The activity involved when the Souls 'take an interest' is somewhat different than, say, when you or I take an interest in something. It is not as if they are picking up a book, or perhaps surfing TV channels or the Web. Instead, when the Souls took interest, they allowed the essence of their beings to merge with the energy from Humanity's thoughts. They metaphorically surfed the slowly spreading ocean of human thought, waiting for that perfect wave that would carry them into our collective minds. Unlike a human surfer, who might tire of the wait after a few hours of paddling about, the Souls have been idling among our thoughts for uncounted millennia. In that time, they have developed a certain understanding of us. Their attention to our thoughts has been common to human reality for so many generations that their existence has become a familiar, if undefined, aspect of our own. The trouble is, save for those rare exceptions, we never cared to notice. The rare exceptions weren't much help either, because, when they did sense the presence of the Souls, receptive humans either misunderstood the contact or failed to communicate what they correctly understood to others (more will be said about this later).

Though people in general have failed to notice the aspects of the Souls in their lives as such, there has developed a base attitude that there is "something" there. That "something" lies just beyond the lens of clear definition, but our awareness of it is manifest in many forms anyone might find familiar. For instance, hope, inspiration, genius, and an instinct to accept the supernatural are a few manifestations of our sense of the Souls, on the positive side. Of course, the existence of this commonality drifting at the edges of our perception led to many often destructive aspects of the human condition. A few examples of the negative side are ethnic/racial divides, nationalism, and a sense that humans, just for being human, are above the general fray of nature, and therefore exempt from its rules.

Positive, negative, or neutral, the Souls never intended to influence human history – eternal beings have little interest in such things – but their presence and our curiosity elevated their influence in our lives long before we could possibly understand the existence, much less the true purpose, of this influence. So we invented our explanations. Well-meaning humans formed religions, nations, entire class systems around their sense of the Souls, all the time simply assuming that this is the way things are, and on an individual basis never questioning that niggling little feeling in the backs of our minds that there must be an explanation beyond the pronouncements of inattentive priests and philosophers (There will be more on why we invent explanations for the presence of the Souls rather than truly identify them later).

The Souls see their effect on the human psyche as neither positive nor negative. The nature of their existence precludes an interest in such things. Besides, to them the effect was one of simple exposure…as though they were exhaling on us, and causing so many spiritual tidbits to wash over us with each ethereal breath. What, really, could be done about it? So they accepted the inevitability of their impact and patiently waited for an aware individual to recognize their existence without bias, rationalization, or fear.

Being individuals themselves, each Soul generates a unique sphere of influence. Call it definition, character, even manipulation, but in truth it is as close to personality as the Souls get – and humans feel it. Because the Souls' specific personality traits do not interfere with each other, they tend to gravitate into their own, geographic, spheres of influence. This could explain the remarkably different manner in which people who share virtually identical DNA, creation myths, and general moral values can feel so different culturally. Compare Asians, Europeans, Africans, Native Americans, Arabs, Indians, and Slavs. Wonder at their similarities, but then wonder at their ability to find difference between each other. Being humans who are not aware of the Souls, this difference is amplified and generalized into palpable things, like competition, mistrust, and hate.

Though the Souls' matrix of being encompasses the entire universe, they do so in harmonic unison, which would explain how all seven are manifest on our single little planet. That matrix is vast and in constant flux, so, even though the presence of all seven exists everywhere, aspects of one might bubble to the surface of human behavior on one occasion, only to fade and be replaced by another Soul's traits some time later. Historians notice the flux as they review the rise and fall of global civilizations, religions, and societal norms. Those changes in power and human interest are simply reflections of each Soul as it drifted to prominence in the collective human psyche. The historians, of course, never quite record it that way.

Human history was not the sole recipient of these fluctuations. The Souls cast their influence upon several races that achieved sentience at other times in earth's history. Most dramatic was the race we call raptors, who dwarfed humans in thought energy production and creative intellect just as they dwarf humans in size. The raptors were in open sentient contact with the Souls for millennia, but in their arrogance, they never felt a need to assist the Souls. They held to this in spite of the warning the Souls gave them about an approaching asteroid, which allowed the raptors an extra millennium to prepare their exit from earth. The raptors to this date thrive elsewhere in the galaxy, advance, civilized, and completely disinterested in aiding the very beings responsible for their existence. The Souls, of course, care nothing about the raptors' negligence; such emotion is not in them. Indeed, the prophet says that the Souls to this day leave a door propped open for them: the prophet says he has even met his raptor counterpart – an experience that left him humbled and, briefly, quite shaken.

Other sentient races who were aware of the Souls include the ant colonies and cetaceans. The ant colonies gave the Souls much hope, initially, but as the individual colonies evolved in intelligence and spirituality, it became clear that the ant colonies' self-styled ascension outweighed any assistance the Souls may have provided. The prophet insists that the ant colonies were wrong about this, and, had they bound their thoughts to the Souls, they would have achieved much more than the advanced state of existence that they currently enjoy. Considering that an ant colony enjoys virtual immortality, freedom, and is impervious even to human attack (remember that one ant colony can be the physical size of a small human country), such a claim means a lot; the ant colonies are the most contemplative beings the Souls have ever encountered on earth, but since the ants have chosen to forego learning to manipulate the vast amounts of thought energy they produce, they have forever abandoned a chance to transcend into beings equal to the Souls in scope and ability. Humans are far below the ant colonies in intellectual power, but they seem to the Souls to be more open to transcendence than the ants, and thus have the potential to become vastly more successful than the ants, in the end.

The cetaceans had more tenuous contact with the Souls. Though sentient, they never allowed themselves to fully grasp either the nature of the Souls or their own spiritual and intellectual capacity. Instead, they allowed their society to devolve to its current state of simple swimming ease before the Souls could encourage their participation.

Each of these three groups could fill volumes, were historians privy to the many, many encounters and intellectual exchanges they had with the souls. The same could be said for humans, as much of the Souls' intentional contact with us took place in our own prehistory, though we obviously gleaned little from it, save a rich foundational mythology that has served as the basis of all modern religions and much of our secular culture. Sadly, humanity had no idea where it was getting their "ideas," so any chance of associating their visions to the Souls was lost to the "here & now" power of priests and shamans.

So the Souls, adrift in this physical universe sans rudder, wind, or favorable current, continued to seed human dreams with archetypical imagery and then waited. And waited.

They still wait, their glacial patience tempered only by the ominous fact that this expanding universe that imprisons them will fade in a few billion years, so, for them, time is short. They are not panicked, as such emotion does not exist in their realm (though it does serve to entertain them as they observe other races throughout the universe destroy themselves through irrational ephemeral fear). However, as biological beings reach their apexes everywhere, with no replacements (as humans "replaced" the raptors, for instance) in sight, they are concerned that humanity may be their final hope. We might be the last chance they have to regain cohesion, to return to eternal perfection. Our reward for helping them may be opportunity to touch that perfection, perhaps even to join it. Assuming enough of us ever pay enough attention to get their message!

The first humans to make honest contact with a Soul in modern times were the primordial practitioners of Hindu, approximately five thousand years ago. Though this was about the same time that Souls touched early Hebrew prophets, the Hebrews were too quick to mystify their encounters to call those early communications mature. The same was true for the Egyptian priests: though their self-centered interpretations of encounters with the Souls were far more creative and archeologically entertaining, they amounted to nothing for the Souls, and added very little to human spiritual development in general. The Hindus, however, allowed their awareness to accept the souls and welcome them into their experience. Sadly, there were still too many materialistically ambitious Hindu priests who failed to understand the Souls but did understand worldly power. They usurped the flirtation and built the Hindu religion directly upon the framework of the Souls. An enduring religion that included much reference to the Souls emerged, but in time Hindu forgot its roots, and the Souls were replaced by more colorful, easily understood gods. Another opportunity for the Souls was lost to human creativity.

There were a few other close calls, as history ebbed and flowed: Moses, Buddha Plato, Jesus, King Arthur (yes, he was real), Copernicus, Shakespeare, DaVinci, Locke, Newton, Tesla, Woodrow Wilson, Ghandi, Martin Luther King, and many more were touched by the souls but, lacking proper metaphor to define them, chose to redefine their encounters into something different. Their interpretations were certainly good for human development, but not too helpful for the souls.

It wasn't until the 20th century and a combination of two unlikely events that the souls would find their moment of communication improved. Those events were the emergence of Einstein and his theories, and the two World Wars (which, from the Souls' perspective, and more than a few historians as well, were actually just one very long conflict).

Though Einstein was really the pinnacle of a new way of perceiving the physical universe shared by many powerful minds, it was his simple equation, $e=mc^2$, that changed forever the fundamental parameters of human experience, society, and, above all, thought. Einstein begat relativity, which begat quantum mechanics, which combined to allow a thinking human's expectations to expand beyond what all of his ancestors believed as rote truth. That there was potentially more "out there" than we could perceive right now became a given in intellectual thought, a notion that a century previously would have seemed oxymoronic. [Due to the author's woeful lack of mathematical skills, Einstein's theories, quantum mechanics, and theoretical physics will not be discussed specifically here. Plenty of others have done so, and the reader is encouraged to research them – all Souls aside, the modern world is driven by Einstein's postulates; to understand them, even vaguely, is good prep work for enduring the changes coming in the near future.]

This new, seemingly more sensible but mysterious way of perceiving and explaining reality coexisted with twenty years of the most destructive behavior humanity has ever expressed. With the World Wars came a new, existential sense of nihilism that competed directly with and threatened to transform Einstein's revelations into something very bad. Indeed, the arrival and use of the atomic bomb seared humanity philosophically, leaving a scar on our collective psyche that has yet to heal. But that searing proved to have a cleansing effect as well, in that it caused thinking humans to lean less on established religious and philosophical tenets when they inevitably searched beyond themselves for more. Three generations later, this is the norm in even the least of thinkers: pop culture, for instance, abounds with science fiction, magic, and superheroes. Sure, the non-thinkers who tend to rely on religion for metaphysical foundation still exist, but their power to automatically influence all human thought, to define the metaphors, as it were, has waned dramatically. This core shift in the way we see ourselves has altered the way we see our dreams. Lucid dreaming, or the ability to be aware that we are having a dream *during* that dream, entered the popular culture at this point. Had Einstein and the World Wars never happened, that probably would not have happened, and the Souls would still be without a connection to human thought; still waiting.

Yes, Einstein and Hitler inadvertently worked together to allow humans to understand that they can lucid dream, and accept possibilities related to it. Now, one might ask whether the Souls had something to do with *causing* Einstein and the wars. This author hopes not, but, given the Souls' disinterest in human events or moralities, such behavior, though perhaps beyond them physically, is not beyond them morally.

So, after millions of years of patiently monitoring the development of sentient life on earth (and elsewhere in the universe, of course), one group has finally shown real potential for both communicating with the Souls and helping them regain their natural existence. That group is humanity and, though contact has been nascent at best, it has begun, through their interaction with the prophet, and his with all of us.

The Prophet

As the Souls cannot naturally communicate with humans, so too humans cannot communicate with the Souls. It is not entirely true that humans are incapable of communing with the Souls: we are all experiencing an exchange with the Souls at some level at all times. We are simply unaware, generally, that a conversation is taking place. In other words, communication is not impossible, just unnatural. As stated earlier, another unique aspect of humanity that is unnatural is thought. When combined with thought, heightened awareness does give humans a glimpse of the Souls. That glimpse is fleeting, like peripherally spotting a small animal in a field while speeding in a car. We know that we saw something out there, somewhere, but it is gone before we can perceptually nail it down, and the whole encounter is forgotten shortly after. The Souls existence, though fundamental to the universe itself, is completely removed from any kind of natural understanding. Human existence also includes certain aspects, like thought and self-awareness, which elude valid natural understanding. Though the Souls and humanity seem to be traveling down the same road, they are doing so at different speeds. One of the drivers, humanity, has no natural reason to look anywhere but straight down the highway, and then only exactly as far as needed to avoid an accident. Humans have no natural vehicle for spotting their fellow travelers. Though we do have the 'unnatural' vehicles in self-awareness and reason, those tools are not tuned to the same frequency as the Souls' message. So we miss it, even when it is spoken directly into our spiritual ears.

Spiritually speaking, a Soul's presence could be drifting directly alongside an honestly aware human, and that human will still not correctly identify it. This is because humans lack a metaphor to assimilate the nature of the Souls (who, by the way, do not use metaphor to understand their reality) into their minds. This absence of a baseline for assimilation represents an enormous hurdle for the Souls, because humans cannot exercise true cognition without metaphor. The Souls came to accept, after uncounted millennia, that they could not practically contact all humans on their own. They required an avatar, an individual who understood them (the Souls), and could paint a picture of that understanding to his people. As the Souls struggled (assuming that beings existing outside time and space can actually struggle) to find this person, they encountered many who came close, but misinterpreted the Souls' message as a religious encounter, or, worse, failed to present a usable metaphor at all, and chose instead to invent a new religion in order to explain their experience in human terms. They did this with the best intentions, but that did not make the chronic miscommunication any better. Jesus, among others, had this problem to a degree, or rather suffered from it: though he understood the Souls' message and did his best to disseminate it with some truly original metaphor, his followers still could not grasp his meaning. Instead of learning about the Souls, they did their best to attach widely accepted metaphor to Jesus' words and created, against Jesus' wishes, Christianity.

In earth's case (remember that the Souls' search encompasses our entire universe, and we are by no means alone, though the author tends to lean anthropo-centric for simplicity's sake), the Souls had to wait until the 20th century before the correct combination of awareness, imagination, and attention occurred in a single human who could be deemed their avatar; their prophet. Though the word 'prophet' is weighted by history with certain religious connotation that perhaps is not relevant here, the Souls and the prophet himself feel that this word most accurately represents his activity, and the Souls' interests.

Ironically, this confluence happened in the mind of a person who had no interest in or aspiration toward a concept like the Souls. It was a lucid dreamer who would become the Soul's prophet.

One might ask why it took so long for a prophet to be designated, when humans have been lucid dreaming for millennia. The difficulty the Souls encountered up until then was quite simple and universal: the rest of the confluence was missing. Sure, a person may have been able to draw his awareness into a dream with him, but for almost all of human history when that happened, the person was unable to transcendentally interpret his experience, and tended to attach a metaphor that already existed within his experience. The attached metaphor was usually religious in nature, though some other fascinating interpretations emerged in the nineteenth century involving ESP, ghosts, and similar phenomena that these romantic science-oriented visionaries used in place of religious symbols that they knew would not fit, or were out of vogue. Most dreamers lacked the imagination (with a few noted and later misunderstood exceptions) to interpret, in a human manner, the Souls. The highest-profile failed prophet of the last century was Carl Jung, who actually created an entire class of metaphor encased firmly in contemporary psychology to explain his experience – he sat right on the Souls' front porch, but refused to believe, or publicly extol, the presence of a fundamental being older and perhaps more universally encompassing than the God in whom he wished to believe. Jung, and all before him, lacked the imagination necessary to truly understand the Souls and their message. Jung did, just as ironically, implant with his philosophy an innate cognitive foundation in future generations that helped, along with other changes in the human psyche mentioned earlier, to nurture the necessary imagining in the prophet, who finally surfaced at the end of the twentieth century.

This prophet was a fairly common human by any measure, save that he had an almost consuming interest in lucid dreaming. Lucid dreaming is simply described as the act of carrying waking-life self-awareness into one's dreams. In other words, a lucid dreamer brings his waking life Self into a dream, and remembers that his actual physical form is sleeping somewhere outside this dream. Plenty of people predating the prophet shared his curiosity about dreaming, but those dreamers chose to attach existing metaphor to their lucid experiences, or, worse, sought to define their awareness of their dreams with terms provided to them by the unimaginative but much revered contemporary human intellectual elite. This was the same block that the Souls encountered when Tibetan Buddhists raised their awareness to the point of interweaving their very consciousnesses with the Souls. However the Tibetans, like later western materialists, chose to interpret their experience according to rules provided them by others rather than seek new metaphor, new explanation, by allowing transcendent explanations to enhance their imaginations (even transcendence is explained by the Tibetan monks, which by definition is impossible; more on that later). The prophet had no interest in accepted wisdom; he just liked to immerse his self-awareness into the limitless world of his dreams. As he developed his ability, he found that the dream itself no long mattered – he only cared about the presence of his awareness in the dream state. In time he abandoned the dreams that his physical mind provided, and endeavored to have lucid dreams with no content, save his awareness.

The man's -- the author assumes the prophet is, or was, a man, since that is the way that he has defined himself to others. It could of course be otherwise -- dream exercises raised the attention of the Soul who incidentally permeated his being. Following an eons-old protocol, that Soul reached out with its message of presence and need. The man, adrift in the nothingness of an image-free but awareness-heavy lucid dream, felt the message. Not knowing initially what to make of it, he reacted in a most peculiar, for humanity, way: *he listened.* He quietly paid attention, offering no input from his personal experience or explanation from his intellect, and let his Soul's message be 'spoken' without daring to interpret, identify, or qualify it. What happened next was impossible, by human scientific standards: the man's awareness transcended his own existence, his own ability to understand, and he comprehended the Soul's plea. The man, by patiently attending to the phenomena unfolding around his psyche, was able to bind to a new metaphor that portrayed a reality beyond anything in proscribed nature to explain the message of the Soul. In the instant that he spent allowing his awareness to pay attention to experience beyond human ken, he became the Soul's avatar for humanity. Just as quickly the man gained a full understanding of his mission and a unique ability to minister this mission to his species. He became the prophet.

Though he sensed his selection, and knew that he was part of something truly primordial, the dreamer's role as prophet was initially ill-defined at best. The Souls' method of communication resides outside of time (where it was formed), so it sometimes is ponderously slow, sometimes impossibly fast, and always laden with vast chunks of information that is both incomprehensible and irrelevant to humans. Their conversations with the prophet were also utterly devoid of handy expediters like instructions, tenets, or even a simple mission statement. Confined to his own intellect and imagination, the prophet independently developed an interpretation that he assumed properly conveyed both the existence of the Souls and revealed a path that could be followed to understand and finally fulfill their long-held intention. This man, this avatar, was able to do this, and to stretch his mind even further to develop a coherent rationale for why it was worth humanity's time to help the Souls. No raptor ever managed that!

Over the course of several years and several thousand lucid dreams the prophet learned the history, plight, and power of the Souls. The Souls provided without hesitation all of the information the prophet could glean, though that gleaning amounted to a vast cauldron of knowledge from which he had to sip ever so daintily, lest he be overwhelmed and risk burying himself with delusions concocted from fear or awe. Somehow he knew that those delusions must be identified and avoided because they might cause *him* to conjure a new religion, rather than to fashion a bridge between humanity and the Souls, a bridge whose crossing might also help attentive humans to locate and develop their own souls, leading possibly toward an opportunity to enjoy eternal life (more later). He did come close a few times to lending mundane definition to what he was learning, but he managed to meter his awareness in a manner that rejected "given" tenets of deity, glory, and salvation, thus leaving his own cognitive door open to what the Souls were really sharing. He avoided the traps to which many before him had succumbed, including the uniquely human penchant for naming one's self a deity. He was also careful to avoid dovetailing the Souls' message into his current religion or tribal belief. Above all, he did not dismiss the Souls' message as just another hallucination brought on by his ill-tempered imagination.

And so, many, many dreams later, the prophet finally possessed the spiritual and intellectual wherewithal to readily engage the Souls, to become a door for the rest of humanity, propped slightly ajar in their dreams with the light and message of the Souls shimmering just behind that tiny opening. With this access, the Souls could communicate within their own terms, tapping parameters that exist outside of space and time, and the prophet could understand and translate. After that, things happened very quickly from our point of view: In the space of one human dream (thirty minutes, perhaps), the Souls communicated their plan for return to their own reality, and humanity's place in that scheme.

Little is known of the prophet's waking life after the intervention of the Souls. There is an excellent chance that he simply walked away from waking life completely, intent as he was on sharing the Souls message. Indeed, he has hinted to those who would listen and understand that his physical form has been neglected for so many decades that, even if family members from his corporeal life had once tried to sustain it, his original human body is likely long gone. In a sense, the prophet's existence is one of perpetual dream, though the dreams he now experiences are not his own, but those of any and all humans. This existence, this exposure in both directions to the dreams of individual humans and the thoughts of the Souls, is what defines him as the prophet.

So defined, we can now take a closer look at how the prophet sees to his mission; how he attempts, constantly, to communicate to those who will listen.

The prophet's stated mission is familiar to those who have encountered him: to encourage as many humans as possible to pay attention to the message of the Souls, that they (individual humans) might work with them (the Souls) to free the Souls and clear the path for the next step in human evolution. Specific details of the Souls' message, what human work is necessary, and what our reward might be, have been sketchy at best, and certainly not agreed upon by the folks who to date have woken from lucid dreams that included the prophet, his message, but no clear key to interpreting it into human terms. So, needless to say, the prophet's mission has only just begun.

He became aware fairly early in his oneiric 'rounds' that simply appearing in dreams and shouting, "Pay attention!" is not adequate communication, especially when that shout is made in the context of another person's chaotic apparently symbol-ridden dream. Lucid or not, a dreamer is going to be inclined to attach meaning that the prophet never implied, and create explanations that the prophet never provided, simply because that is what even the most enlightened of dreamers do. With some consultation from the Souls (whose experience in this is vast), the prophet adopted a routine nested in patience and careful subtlety, rather than a more direct and potentially misinterpreted approach.

The prophet completes each journey not by seeking but by waiting. He allows his awareness to ride the gentle waves of the Souls' thought energy as it permeates the minds of all sleeping people. With that he is able to establish a small foothold in almost every sleeper's dreamscape. His presence is minimal, but always detectable, in every dream. Once in, he waits for the dreamer to detect his presence. Should he be discovered, the prophet begins his work with glacially administered care. This is because his 'foothold' is defined not by the prophet but by each dreamer, and he could appear to the dreamer as almost any object or creature the dreamer can imagine. The prophet has no interest in trying to relay the Message of the Ages while manifest as a light switch, an old girlfriend, or perhaps a squirrel. Instead of communicating directly, he works to raise the profile of his adopted image until the dreamer more than *notices* him (or rather his current form), but attaches *significance* to his presence. Once that occurs, and the prophet sees the dreamer is on his spiritual page, he attempts to communicate. This is a difficult task on its face, since even the most imaginative dreamer might not react well to a light switch starting up a chat. But it does work occasionally, and when it does, the prophet will try to make his point quickly, using as few potentially misinterpreted words as possible.

What does he say? Well, it could be almost anything, or nothing at all. He avoids saying the same thing every time for fear that those repeated words will become an archetypical metaphor in themselves, and, soon enough, hopeful dreamers will be dreaming of an idyllic young man (or woman, as it were) proclaiming those words backed by the most impressively spiritual images possible...and it would be 'just a dream.' The dreaming mind is a master at providing the dreamer precisely the image she desires – most 'lucid' dreams are in fact not lucid at all, but rather regular dreams *about* being lucid – while real awareness remains neatly tucked away. So the prophet measures the awareness levels of the lucid dreamer, surveys the dream the lucid dreamer has assembled, and determines then what message is best to project. It could be words, it could be images, or even simply feelings, but his message will be perceived by the dreamer as something truly different (as in, not from the dreamer's own mind), something very important, and something that essentially instructs him to pay attention, next time. Should the dreamer successfully take this message into waking life, and works to prepare her mind for the "next time," then the prophet will be sure to present himself in her next lucid dream, and will converse more openly. His message at first will be quite simple. Regardless of the dreamer's level of preparedness; the prophet has no interest in burying the dreamer with an in-depth lore of the Souls, their plight, and humanity's potential remedy. That would be too much information for the dreamer to process, likely resulting in the dreamer producing an exciting but useless mythology from existing earthly metaphor to both explain his encounter and perhaps to start yet another redundant religion. Instead the prophet will reinforce the dreamer's unavoidable expectations with images, and perhaps words, that grow what the dreamer wants to hear into a palatable message that the prophet wants to instill. This process can happen in one dream or take years, but it must occur before the prophet can attempt to recruit the dreamer to the Souls' cause. Once the process has been fully run through, and the dreamer can recognize the prophet in his dream, hear what the prophet has to say, and is able to absorb transcendental imagery, then the prophet can move ahead with more complex instruction.

This to date has never happened, but the prophet is patient, and well aware that his mission has just begun, and will likely span many years; perhaps centuries. In the meantime, he continues to appear in people's dreams, generally in a random fashion, and projects from his post as light switch, old girlfriend, or whatever, an image of hope, promise, and, if the dreamer is truly paying attention, camaraderie. Above all right now the prophet seeks to instill in as many dreamers' minds as possible that there really is "more" out there, and that that more can be obtained, appreciated, and grown simply by an initial act of paying attention. So in the end the prophet can be described as an entity who wanders the realm of dreaming in search of human dreamers able and willing to pay enough attention to his message of aid to the Souls. There is no doubt more to the prophet's mission, but it has not yet been shared. As far as we know, he exists only to find a way to merge the human groupmind with that of the Souls. By doing that, the Souls will somehow free themselves of their imprisonment in this universe while simultaneously leaving that group of attentive humans a legacy of their experience, knowledge, ability, and some enlightenment about their own spiritual potential.

Some techniques thought to raise a dreamer's awareness and receptivity to the prophet have been developed over the years, and will be discussed elsewhere in this book. For now suffice it to say that if you are an accomplished lucid dreamer with a powerful sense of self, you will likely encounter the prophet in your dreams. But that encounter will go unnoticed by you even then, should you fail to pay attention.

First Dream Encounter: Ashley

I was in the middle of a tiresome dream involving yet another violent argument with my five brothers and sisters when I noticed that my little sister Ellie was a ninety-year-old woman struggling with a walker beside me. Recognizing the oddity, I told myself that this was a dream, bid my bruised and bewildered sib-characters farewell and did what I always do when lucid: I took flight.

I was soaring high in a perfect blue sky, nude, alone, and in as near a state of bliss as I can achieve. The ocean, dotted with green islands, shimmered in perfect postcard blue far below me.

I had done this before, many times, and was ready for a good twenty minutes of wonderful freedom, far from my husband, my kids, and all of waking life's troubles. I wondered if this time the trip might be followed by a stop on one of those islands far below for a romantic interlude with that hunk from page 34 of last month's Cosmo. Then something very different happened.

I was flying with great velocity, enjoying the cool breeze that flowed over my body, as if cleansing it. I looked down the length of each of my outstretched arms (arms that had regained their 19-year-old firmness, I am delighted to add), as I was wont to do mid flight, and my review was met with that something different: an eagle was soaring just a few inches to the right of my splayed, perfectly manicured right-hand fingertips.

This never happened before, I thought to myself. The eagle was huge, bigger than I was, and it was almost completely white, save for a black head and neck (a negative of an American bald eagle, I suppose – I wondered what that meant, briefly). It matched my every move, even when I challenged it with tight loops and barrel rolls. I was impressed, but also very confused. What was this big bird doing in *my* dream, anyway? Was I having some twisted Jonathan Livingston Seagull moment? Was the bird going to tell me how much I could become if only I acted just like it did? God I hope not was all I could think. Then the eagle looked right at me, its eyes suddenly very human and very blue. I could have sworn it was smiling at me, all beaks aside. Then, it spoke.

"Ashley," it said softly; too softly to be heard, if we had been flying in the real world, "Should I not have come?"

"It's okay with me, as long as your name isn't Jonathan or Richard," I replied before I could stop myself.

"No worries there miss, though I must admit that I might have had some influence in that story too."

"Why are you flying next to me like that?"

"Should I not be?"

"Well, for all intents and purposes I'd say no you shouldn't. This is my dream, you know."

"Yes I do."

"Yes you do what? Have a right to be in my dream, or something else?"

"Let's go with 'something else' for now, Ashley. Hey, my feathers are getting tired. Can we stop and chat on the ground?"

"Do I have a choice?"

"Of course you do; I mean seriously, it is your dream."

I actually did think about it for a moment, if even that long. After all, I said to myself, it was my dream. Why should I do its bidding? And how the hell do feathers get tired, anyway? But then, sure enough, I said:

"I suppose I do. There is an island about which I had always been fond. We could land there."

"Sounds good."

"Okay then…just don't get too excited if some hunk with great hair shows up looking for me with his hands."

"I won't"

"And don't eat him!"

"Not a chance."

Then another thing that had never happened before did: We were suddenly standing on that very familiar beach, sans my hairy dreambeau Hans. We did not even have to land.

"Of course not," the eagle said, pecking at his wings, "Mind if I change into something more comfortable now, so we can chat?"

"Go for it – but I have a lunch date at noon, just so you know."

"Understood," the man said. I could say 'the man said,' now, because the eagle had morphed into a youthful human male, brown hair, blue eyes, good build, cheap but satisfactorily tight clothes. He was smiling, his face golden in the late afternoon sun. Suddenly self-conscious, I looked down to confirm that I was no longer naked. To my relief, I was dressed – somewhat, at least: I wore that tight red cocktail dress that got me into so much trouble at the last company Christmas party.

"Well, good," I said, "Why don't you tell me what the hell you're doing in my dream? Because you know it's my dream, don't you?"

"I guess the real question is, do *you* know?"

"Of course I do. This is a dream. Only a dream. My dream."

"Then why am I here?"

"That's a bizarre question coming from you. Shouldn't it be mine to ask?"

"I suppose it should," he said, admiring the sun that had paused mid-set on the horizon, bathing my dream beach in my favorite soft golden light. In a moment he said, "Are you going to?"

"Um, sure. Why are you here?"

"Isn't this your dream? Shouldn't you know?"

"Hey! That's not fair!"

"But either way it's true," he said, with a sad face that fought to obscure the twinkle in his eye, "This is your world, not mine. I'm just visiting."

"Why? Or do I have to know that too?"

"Well, you did tell me that it is your dream…"

"Oh, come on!"

"Hey lady, I just work here," he said. It was obvious I wasn't going to be told why he was in my dream. It seemed I would have to tell him. But I did not know, and he seemed to acknowledge that with an almost imperceptible pout of his now gray eyes. He shrugged, looked out at the now setting sun, and said, "Oh, Ashley, you're so close, yet so very very far. I'll be gone now, but do your best to remember me, remember yourself, and in time I'll no doubt be back for you, with bells on."

"Bells," I repeated, suddenly very, very sad. I don't like being sad, especially in dreams, and began to wonder if it wasn't time to wake up.

"Nah," he said, touching my extended hand, "Fly some more. Be free. Shout for Hans. Enjoy yourself. But all the while, don't forget who you are, and pay attention! When you do both well, I'll be here, and you'll understand. Hell, I'll be here anyway, but at least then we'll both care."

"Huh?" I asked. He was gone before my words echoed softly over the empty sand. In a moment, so was the beach. I was flying again, free again, but for some reason I kept looking over my right fingertips until I awoke, and even after, feeling very different but very very sadly the same.

Thought Energy

Though it forms the very matrix of the Souls' existence in our universe, elevates sentient beings (including humanity) above the terms and conditions of physical reality, and was the inadvertent mortar that binds our successful universe, thought energy is not tapped, understood, studied, or even theorized about by modern humanity. That is because, by humanity's rules, thought is an abstract term, and cannot exist as an energy form.

That thought energy cannot currently be empirically studied or mathematically formulated is a real game-ender for scientists. Also, because it is not compatible with the rest of the physical universe, there is little chance that the scientific community as we know it can or will ever take an interest in identifying and quantifying thought energy. That leaves the mystics. Though *they* have certainly been creative in their defining of thought energy over the centuries (i.e., theology, magic, prayer, cosmic energy, vibration, etc), their definitions lean more toward crowd-pleasing imaginative inventions than they do toward accurately describing a subject that is quite simple, even while defying mathematics.

What is thought energy? Before we go there, we should clarify quickly what thought energy is *not*: it is not the same as brain waves, or the electromagnetic forces produced by the activity of neurons. That is a different sort of energy related directly to the natural world as created by the Eighth Soul's Big Bang. That kind of biomechanical energy is generated by all animals to some degree, regardless of sentience. Though it is quite real and has great value to science, it is not what we are talking about here, and it should not be confused with thought energy. Ever. That said, we can ask more readily: what is thought energy?

In the simplest of terms, it is the force created from nothing more than the event of a conscious thought. In the most complex of terms, it is the force created from nothing more than the event of a conscious thought. That there is no complexity, and that thought energy fails to conform to mathematic analysis, pretty much erases it from any lexicon of modern physics. That is fair, because by any measure, and by all the rules as provided by nature itself, thought energy cannot exist.

In truth it is the other way around: the one single pure form of energy *is* thought energy, as it was the only form of energy generated by the Eight Souls *before* our universe was created by the ambitious Soul. When it launched the universe, it invented and applied all those laws of physics we hold absolute by drawing from the only energy source available to it: the well of its thought energy. In a real sense that creator-Soul's cataclysmically irrational thoughts were the progenitors of all those inexplicably rational, calculable laws of physics.

What can thought energy do, other than trigger a big bang? Though it is a very weak force, thought energy can do quite a bit, thanks to its unique nature. Because it exists outside of the laws of physics, thought energy is both exempt from those laws and able to affect them dramatically. Like a pin popping a balloon, thought energy will jam itself into the matrix of any physical system and can potentially disrupt or change that system simply by being present...sort of like adding a new letter to $E=mc^2$. Being thinking beings, humans can provide this pin, and they indeed do so, on a regular basis. To date, however, this affectation of human thought has been accidental when initiated by humans or other sentient beings. This is because it is currently not possible for humans to consciously form a thought whose corresponding energy might influence the exact thing that the human wanted to influence. That does not mean that influence doesn't happen; it means that wielders of thought forms (specifically shaped 'pins' that pop the otherwise well-established balloons of natural physical events) have no idea what they are wielding. For instance, a human can create a thought form whose energy signature is just right for, say, changing the specific gravity of a nearby pencil. The pencil floats into the air, and the person sees it happen. Instead of acknowledging that his thoughts had generated just the right energy key to erase a pencil's mass, the thinker decides that he has just experienced a bout of telekinesis. If the thinker has his wits about him, he will remember exactly what thought crossed his mind at the moment the pencil rose, and be able to repeat the action in the future, preferably before an audience. The thinker fails to realize that his thought energy moved the pencil, because the thought he had while moving it was likely not about the pencil. Telekinesis, which does not exist either in science or in the reality of the Souls, will be the chosen phenomenon because there is an available mythology to support an explanation, so the action of the pencil is easier to describe using popular telekinetic terms rather than thought-form terms. In truth, most if not all of what we term supernatural events are directly related to thought forms randomly influencing physical reality.

Thought energy may be responsible for our very existence: As the Souls were expanding through the created universe, they maintained constant communication with each other. This communication was in their pre-big bang format of pure thought energy, and thus failed to follow the eighth's new rules of time and space. Their communication was not without influence, though. As the eons passed, the "lines" of communication between the Souls formed an intricate pattern of pathways throughout our universe. Cosmic rabbit-runs, as it were, laced, connected, and provided a logical, steady web of weak energy to the expanding universe. These rabbit runs may have facilitated the expansion of another very weak force in the Eighth's created physical universe – gravity. As gravity tumbled down these hyper-structured paths of thought energy, it began to assume their patterns as its own and, since gravity is an accumulating force, those patterns consolidated over uncounted eons into the glue that holds the stars and planets together. This is why gravity is so influential in the universe, yet does not fit into the Standard Model, the equation that neatly describes the other three forces and their relationship to physical reality.

Now we arrive at the fun part. Thought energy is arguably the most influential force in the universe, only because it *cannot* exist. This influence is exerted by humans all the time, but those who are doing the influencing have no idea that they tapping their own thought energy. They instead blame their influence on fate, luck, God, magic, supernatural forces, or whatever other clever explanation their imagination can conjure. The explanations are usually absurd, but the forces their thoughts create are real, as are the changes in the universe they might be making.

Another interesting aspect of thought energy is that a thought form exists everywhere in the universe, instantly, thanks to the fact that it is not governed by the Standard Model, which includes the $e=mc^2$ speed limit. This is how the prophet can appear in millions of dreams simultaneously, and also how the Souls will eventually be able to work with us, even though they are spread so thinly throughout the universe.

The Seven Souls, who are the very source of thought energy, have told the prophet that as a side effect of helping them, cooperative humans will come to understand the nature of thought forms, and learn how to wield them on purpose. This of course could yield a potentially negative side-effect, as humans will be able to change the rules of physics, and that is not always a good thing. The prophet seems to dismiss this as an immediate danger, though, since the sort of humans (and sentients in general) with whom the Souls choose to communicate with would not by their very nature wish to cause harm to their world. Also he insists that, after the transcendental event of communicating with the Souls strikes a human, she will tend to lose interest in mundane things like altering her local laws of physics.

Finally, the prophet hinted at another long-term aspect of thought energy accessible even to those people who were unable to commune with the Souls: As each thinking person generates a unique thought energy signature – wavelength, as it were, though there is no physical evidence of how the stuff works – they accumulate a pool of thought energy that will exist forever (Newton was apparently right about that). This pool glows forever with all the accumulated thoughts of the person who created it, in a tangible and potentially organized manner. In other words, over their physical human lifetime every thinking person creates his own eternal soul, and the quality of that soul is defined by the quality of the thoughts that accumulate in that pool. As it exists without consciousness or awareness, this soul is essentially a bundle of energy whose signature uniquely matches that of the individual who created them. It is potentially a powerful source of energy to be tapped, perhaps, but it is not sentient on its own. Upon the death of our physical bodies, we have opportunity in our last living moments to dive our consciousness into that pool, and preserve our selves, in energy form, forever. This potential has long been known but always misinterpreted by religions, parapsychologists, and others seeking definition rather than truth. The group who came closest to the truth is the Tibetan Buddhist monks, many of whom dedicate their lives to mastering an ability to maintain their awareness straight through their own deaths. Unfortunately, they think they are doing so to jump off a great wheel of reincarnation rather than lend sentience to their waiting souls, but hopefully they will learn as they, um, go.

That we can activate, perhaps occupy, or at least make sentient the accumulated pool of our lives' thought is the reason that the Souls insist that we be nice to each other, and try to avoid creating hateful or angry thoughts. This is because not only will the energy from those bad thoughts be with us forever, they will provide the makeup of who we are for all eternity. A lifetime accumulation of good, self-aware, and creative thought will create a far more powerful eternal soul than a lifetime of evil, narcissistic, or empty thought (apparently watching reality TV doesn't help much either, the Prophet quipped once). So, eternal life is indeed ours, but it is defined not by a judging God, but by how we lived our corporeal lives…more on that in a later chapter.

There is one group which knows all about thought energy and its byproducts. That group is the Seven Souls. They can not only explain the existence and importance of thought energy, but they can also provide guidelines for forming thoughts that can influence reality, plus an index of sorts of what specific thought forms will do when solicited. This is an enormous opportunity to be had by humanity, should they ever choose to pay attention to the Souls, and their avatar, the prophet. And, even if individuals choose not to pay attention to the Souls, help them, or learn from them, they are still manufacturing during life their own eternal soul, and the makeup of that soul is determined by the quality of their thoughts and actions. So either way, the Souls have revealed that there is indeed something more to our existence than biological humanity, and that something is eternal, and based upon the quality and form of energy generated by our thoughts.

First Dream Encounter: Ted

I was dreaming that I was attending a party, a gathering of hundreds, most of whom I did not know, though I was under the impression that they knew me. The party was being held on the lush back lawn of a palatial estate, and the hour was dusk. I was standing in a circle of six strangers when it suddenly dawned on me that this party was all wrong, that I did not belong, and that I was in fact somewhere else altogether, right now. I was dreaming.

But I was also intrigued. So, after I acknowledged to myself that this was a dream, carefully remembered who I really was, where my physical body was sleeping, etc, I decided to stay at the party and see what significance, if any, all the strange dream characters and the equally alien party locale held.

Though I listened broadly for some time to their conversation, the words emanating from my fellow partiers was babble at best. I was becoming disinterested in the dream as presented. I was about to accept that it was just so much dreck drawn from my overzealous dreaming mind and set about forming a new landscape of my own making when I noticed a horsefly perched on the nose of the particularly attractive young woman standing at about 4 o'clock in my circle.

She did not seem to notice it, nor did any other guest. But it was there, and it had my attention. As it was as big as her nose, my attention was indeed focused! The girl smiled brightly, as if I were heeding her, and not the huge black fly ranging her little button nose. It seemed to pause and regard her wide golden eyes for just a flash before it turned its fidgety little head toward me. When it did I swear it smiled at me, and took off toward me.

I had allowed the bizarre to rule my lucid dream long enough that some of my awareness was ebbing, and I had begun sacrificing lucidity to my dream god. The horsefly seemed to want none of that, and buzzed right at me. As it flitted about me I tried to appear aloof in front of the other guests by coolly ignoring it. However, I couldn't help the occasional peek at it as it orbited my head. Amazingly, when I eyed it squarely, it was not a fly that eyed me back but a black-bearded little man in army fatigues. He tried to speak to me when I saw him, his hovering buzz sounding much like a request in English to let him bite me. He seemed fairly earnest. In response I swatted him, breaking several of his tiny human teeth.

Lucidity returned after that exchange, and I chose this time to leave the building rather than be enthralled again by my dream characters. I chose a red dirt path that formed an exit to the party and the lawn, and walked it slowly. As I did, my dream rapidly shifted to a lush pastoral setting that I have often enjoyed in the past. I turned toward my favorite little mound of fresh-cut grass that I knew would look down on the richest of sunsets, but was visited again by that damn fly. This time, in pure horsefly form, he flew in a great arc around me, circling in until he landed on my neck with a sickening thud. And then he bit me.

That bite startled me into a false awakening that I quickly recognized, as I hadn't left my bed floating in a small blue pond near my pastoral dream scene. I sighed, still a bit flabbergasted at that damn fly-man-thing, and rolled over in my dream bed, wondering what this dream would bring me next, whether I chose to let it in or not.

My question was answered immediately, as the horsefly was lying in the bed beside me. It had grown to my size, and lounged on its back, two sets of legs crossed, one holding a copy of *Catcher in the Rye*. It looked up from its reading as I regarded it. When it did, I saw it was the bearded man again, for just an instant. When it was the horsefly once more and I was about to swat it, it held up a defensive fly-limb that gave me pause. Upon my pause, it spoke:

"Don't swat me bro," was all it said.

"Why not?" I asked, struggling to maintain my awareness, and remember that this was a dream, a dream whose plot and characters were of my making, no matter how odd they might seem.

"That might not be entirely true, Ted," the mini Che Guevara said to me. I was intrigued.

"What do you mean, little fly-man?" I asked, "This is my dream. Everything in it must by definition be mine, too. Right?" The fly-man-thing only sighed and sat up in bed beside me.

"Normally," he said, lighting a character-appropriate cigarette, shaking out the match with yet another available hairy limb, "That is certainly true."

"But not today?" I asked. He seemed to brighten at the question.

"No, Ted, not today," The man said to me, having lost all semblance of flyness seemingly because I opted to give him a chance to speak, rather than just dream-blindly swatting him. He continued, "Today is a little special, because you finally were able to hold your attention long enough to recognize that I was from the outside of your dream world, looking to chat."

"It wasn't so hard to pay attention, Mr. Che Fly Thing. You very much stole the scene at that party."

"You'd be surprised, Ted," he said, "I've been in your dreams many times, in often far more volatile form, and you missed me every time until today."

"That's unbelievable," I said, meaning every word.

"I suppose."

"So, what are you doing here, anyway?"

"Long story. Let's start by having you call me something other than Fly thing. How about Bob?"

A passing real-world fire truck woke me at that instant, ending the encounter, but not my interest in learning more about Bob!

ATTENTION

Since it is the title issue of this book, it might seem odd to the reader that discussion of attention appears to be quite brief. This is because attention is inherently self-explanatory. There is little that can be shared about it that will not elicit a long sigh, and maybe a "duh" or two from the reader.

Attention is the first stage, and certainly the primary driver, of self-awareness. This chapter will focus on this relationship, and will assume that the reader understands the basic definition of attention (being that she has made it to chapter seven of a book like this, she probably does). It will reinforce the fact that attention's primacy in self-awareness is a critical aspect of communication with the Souls.

Attention is a tool used by every living thing, but when tapped by sentient beings it becomes a truly powerful ally. In nature attention is an important tool for self-preservation, as it is the result of any creature's focus on its own environment, perhaps to seek out food, or to avoid becoming food. Because attention is fundamental to the survival of all living things, tapping it is one of the easiest things any living creature can do – any living creature who lacks sentience, that is. This is because sentient beings are able to "think" themselves beyond the basic "fight/flee," "attack/pass" instinctual aspects of attention. They can think in two directions: either focusing more deeply on objects of attention, or intentionally ignoring objects which in nature would demand attention. For instance, anyone driving at 70 mph on the highway does this – any human traveling that fast in most previous generations would have been paying wide-eyed attention to their historically impossible feat of life-threatening velocity; today such motion is downright pedestrian. Because our parents developed the intellectual ability to ignore stimuli that traditionally demanded attention, we have inherited the handicap of inattention. We can choose to ignore. We can choose to allot attention to stimuli that just do not matter, for instance, TV, video games, the latest gossip. As modern society becomes more and more informationally complex, this ignorance tends to lock out far more than it lets in. In time we learn to pay attention only to the things to which we have been trained to pay attention, and we learn to fundamentally ignore anything that is not interesting, foreign to us, or beyond our ken.

Attention exists on many levels, though the Souls and the prophet care little about the levels that are survival-based. They seek intellectual attention, that unique tool of organized and creative thought. From that kind of attention come the Soul-digestible thought-forms that can engage their spheres of perception, and ultimately vise-versa. Also, perhaps as the Souls discover the individual thought forms that can free them, the issuers of those thoughts must be attentive to requests for more, or for refinements (this is an assumption, since the Souls and the prophet have not provided specifics as to how the work will proceed). So the basic levels of attention -- think stone fish patiently waving its bait appendage for hours until a hapless minnow nips at it -- will be ignored here. The level of attention that the Souls require is not necessarily a higher level, and certainly not difficult to achieve; think of it more as a different level. Since the Souls' existence abides a different set of rules than our own, so too then are we obliged to use a different sort of attention to notice them. This attention is based not on senses but on ideas, self-awareness, and, oddly, logic. It is not about focusing senses on an object or situation as much as it is about opening a portion of your self to the possibility that there are more stimuli available to a receptive mind than your natural five senses can perceive. Since the Souls' energy permeates all reality, their stimuli are everywhere around us, and within us. But it takes a focused mind to detect that energy, and a truly disciplined mind to make any sense of it, much less reap its benefits. Of course, that sense-making comes later. First let's focus our attention on, yes, attention.

This book offers no concrete instruction for developing the attention skills necessary to communicate with the Souls. That is because they cannot really be taught: if you are capable of communicating with the Souls, you will need no instruction, and if you are not capable, all the instruction in the world will never work. What this book does endeavor to do, though, is inform readers who have tapped or refined their innate attention skills that there is a valuable use for attention that literally transcends its standard uses, like registering TV, video games, the latest gossip. Hopefully, this book will also stir an interest in developing attention among the many who choose to ignore that which matters. In both cases, the prophet exists to nurture attention. While his primary task is to guide those who are able to pay enough attention to sense him, and have the self-awareness necessary to appreciate the import of his presence, the prophet maintains a presence in the dreams of those who are on the brink of awareness, but might need a little kick.

There are, however, a few basic foundations of attention that must be present to guarantee that real attention can be paid and maintained (all of which are hopefully already old hat to the reader). They are focus, discipline, and imagination.

Focus is genetic. We all have an inherent ability to focus, though that ability may have been clouded by a lifetime of disuse or societal rationalizing (i.e., ADD). If one chooses to exercise her mind to revive innate focusing skills, then she will be rewarded with the ability to focus. This is of course easy to say, but not very easy to do. The laziness that first welcomes and then nourishes the inability to focus is a powerful force, and often very regimented and time-consuming remedies are required to overcome it. Again, there are plenty of books and programs dedicated to those remedies; find the one that works for you, if you know you have discarded your natural ability to focus. This is not the arena for such instruction.

Discipline is probably genetic too, meaning that we all have a capacity for it, but as it is more socially and perhaps genetically buried than focus, and therefore far rarer naturally, discipline is an art better learned from scratch rather than expectation. Discipline is a harsh term in our culture, usually implying much suffering or punitive oversight, but in reality it is simply the mental ability to consistently direct the mind and body toward maintaining focus. Successful athletes are excellent examples of discipline masters – if you know one, ask them how they train, maintain focus, and stick to their goals; should you *pay attention* to their guidance, you will save yourself much time. Discipline is the workhorse of any kind of personal growth. It is the nearly mystical force that pushes you further, compels you to achieve difficult goals and, above all, discipline conditions the psyche to press confidently into unknown territory without fear or self-destruction.

Imagination is not physically genetic, though it is a blessing of sentience that can be nourished by any thinking being with an interest in conjuring the impossible. It is key to recognizing the prophet, accepting the presence of the Souls, and, above all, laying a mental foundation for the transcendental experience of communicating with the Souls and ultimately participating in their realm of existence. Transcendence is impossible without imagination, because by every scientific measure transcendence cannot exist; therefore, one's mind must be open to an experience that cannot be defined by existing scientific or historic metaphor. That means that a person encountering the Souls' plane of existence must define what they see on *completely* new terms, sans traditional metaphor. That takes quite a bit of imagination!

With these three tenets of attention fully mastered, an individual might be able to establish and maintain the awareness necessary to develop their lucid dreaming abilities, and finally notice the presence of the prophet. Of course, that is only the beginning…

First Dream Encounter: Louis

While in the midst of a dream whose details bear no consequence, I became lucid. I quickly gathered my self, and exited the dream provided me. Unfortunately my awareness must not have been complete, because my exit brought me to another dream scene, this time a scene that very much resembled my waking life living room. I concentrated, and as awareness increased I remembered an exercise that I had heard about once regarding the elimination of all things in the dream, leaving nothing but your self, and the dream. I had always wanted to try it, and was feeling quite lucid, so I started subtracting.

First, the large items were dismissed: I watched as the sofa disappeared, as did my recliner, with my wife (or rather a dream character version of her) still aboard. Then the coffee table, the walls, the window (and the scene behind it, which was perhaps the most difficult part of the exercise), the rug, the dog, the floor, etc, faded from my world in rapid succession. In time I was floating in white nothingness, save for one end table and lamp, both of which did not want to disappear.

Well that is just wrong, I thought. So, instead of reveling in my success at emptying the dream scene *almost* completely, or simply turning around and away from my lamp, I focused on it and struggled to make it disappear. It remained; indeed, I was sure that it gained some detail, sharpness, and color. I reminded myself who I was, where I was really (asleep in my bed at home), and what I was looking to do here, and concentrated once more on getting rid of the lamp. My effort seemed only to cause it to cast more light. I yelled at it in frustration, claiming noisily that this was my dream and that that lamp did not belong in it. I swear then that the lamp smiled at me.

This made me laugh, or rather my dream character self laughed, as it threatened to regain a central position in the dream. I fought this, and decided to accept the lamp and table as inexorable parts of my blanked out dream scene. This decision seemed to elevate my awareness, settle me, and I was rewarded by a view of the lamp that I did not have moments earlier: it seemed to be moving slightly, animated as though its glass base were breathing, and its soft yellow light emanated not from its bulb, particularly, but rather from a swarm of tiny comets that orbited the fixture. They moved swiftly, almost invisibly, but they were there; in a very real sense. Like so many electrons around an atom, though, I could not pinpoint them, or stop them long enough to see what they were. Trying to do so, I instinctively felt, would be wrong. So my attention returned to the lamp that they orbited.

That lamp was no longer a light fixture, or table, but a man. He was of medium build and height, with indeterminate features, and I swear his hair and eye color changed every time I reexamined them. He stood where the lamp had been, arms folded, and smiling in a most mischievous way. I rejected the awe and fear I felt at seeing this man, and struggled to accept that here was a person, in my dream, who I had not created. In doing so I was able to maintain my awareness and continue with the experience. I wondered who it was I was looking at. He answered:

"I am simply another dreamer," he said, "Just like you."

"Why are you here?"

"That I can't really say, because my words and time are limited; long story."

"What can you say?"

"Excellent question. I can say I'm here to speak for these, um, comets, I guess, that are swirling around me right now."

"The comets?"

"Well, that's what they are here. But they are so much more, and they ask that, when you are more able, you pay attention to them. They want to make a deal with you."

"What kind of deal?"

"I couldn't say."

"That isn't very fair."

"No really. I couldn't say, because their deal is specific to you, to the very shape of your thoughts. When you are ready, they will ask."

The dream started fading. Rather, the comets disappeared, furniture began reappearing, and the man had become decidedly lamp-like. I was losing lucidity, waking up. I rushed out one more question:

"When am I ready?"

"Don't know. You will. Just pay attention." With that the lamp resumed its inanimate state. It now rested quietly on the table, switched off. My wife looked over from her seat in the recliner, sleepy and curious. With that, the dream faded and I woke up, feeling very tired.

Awareness

Awareness, or more correctly self-awareness, is a key component of sentience, lucid dreaming, interaction with the Souls, and successful transcendence. In other words, it is pretty darn important in the grand scheme of spiritual things. In spite of that, self-awareness remains hands-down the most ignored aspect of consciousness. This is because nature, as created by that eighth Soul, has little to no use for self-awareness in its universe.

Just as nature has no built-in mechanism or formula for thought, it has also omitted self-awareness from its overall "natural" configurations. Why indeed would the natural world want any living creature to realize its presence in reality, or what effect that presence has on its fellow creatures? That would only serve to gum up the works, as it were. Nature, to date, has won the argument, given that self-awareness as a constant condition is a rarity in almost all living things, including sentient beings. Especially humans.

Awareness is a state of consciousness wherein the conscious mind acknowledges the presence of stimuli in an intellectual rather than existential manner. An aware person not only sees, hears, and feels the things going on around him, but also knows that he *is* one of those things too. A self-aware person takes this a step further by understanding that anything he does will have an effect on the world around him. Self-awareness is an almost visceral activity, as it lends real credence to experience, enhancing and making singularly important the stimulus-response version of awareness that nature provides (aka: primitive attention).

Unfortunately self-awareness is not a gift that can be handed out by the prophet or the Souls. Its existence, and recognition of that existence, stems from only one place: individual sentient consciousness. Though by definition awareness (and by extension self-awareness) is a simple thing, it can be difficult to achieve and maintain. In these times of ceaseless mental diversion and compression of billions of lives into a smaller and smaller world, moments of simple self-reflection can truly be rare. Individuals tend to find it difficult, perhaps unnecessary, to realize that their presence has an impact on everything around them, and vise-versa. To not only recognize that condition but to focus on it and use it as a tool for growth is far beyond most people's interest – but it is well within everyone's abilities. Though it is true that self-awareness must be nurtured by the individual, its potential exists in all of us, from the beginning. So I take back what I wrote moments ago: perhaps it *was* a gift. Self-awareness might be an inadvertent addition to our nature, as provided by that eighth Soul billions of years before humans, or life, existed. Or, perhaps the Eighth Soul actually understood the ramifications of his actions, and thus wove a potential for sentience into the fabric of his plans -- just to have a rescue option available, should things go wrong for it. We will never know for sure.

More will be discussed later about the specifics of self-awareness in lucid dreaming. Suffice it to say now that self-awareness is integral to lucid dreaming, and lucid dreaming is a requirement for communicating with the prophet. It can also be said now that an interested party (no disciples, initiates, accolades, or other religious monikers here, thank you) with strong self-awareness during a lucid dream will be well positioned to recognize the prophet and converse intelligently with him. If you are self-aware, you will understand during the dream encounter with the prophet not only the significance of his presence, but also the significance of your own – and that is what will make the difference.

Though self-awareness is a prerequisite for lucid dreaming, its importance does not stop there. Self-awareness provides the mortar for the cognitive bridge necessary to transcend to the level of consciousness demanded for communication with the Souls. That bridge's bricks are memory, and a human that masters both will be well prepared to imagine the new metaphors necessary to truly transcend to a new plane of existence that includes communication with the Souls.

These sentences are vague, and without instruction or obvious definition, but in the end neither is necessary – the Souls merely ask that you rise above yourself and your current expectations of reality for the briefest of times. After that, you will be privy to a plan and a world that both exceed anything any human has ever imagined *and* fit perfectly into the natural rhythm of human evolution. Ironically, the tools for achieving that "natural" evolution – thought, self-awareness, and sentience – are the very tools about which all our sciences' physical models, formulas, and structures care little to nothing. Almost as if it were a defense mechanism unconsciously contrived by the eighth Soul, self-awareness exists despite the rules against it. Its existence is the only thing, in the end, that will elevate human minds to a level wherein they can talk to, and help restore the eighth's siblings.

First Dream Encounter: Howard

I was up in that tree on that hill, again. The giant yellow T-rex, the same monster as it was a thousand times since I was seven, had just cocked his head my way and would soon come to nip at me, again, when I remembered that this was a dream. Immediately I felt better about my situation, but, instead of leaving the dream or turning the yellow monster into a yipping puppy (as was my wont of late), I paused for a second: the T-rex, I noticed, had already done the same. It had stopped its snarling and simply stood there, just below the bottom branch of my leafless tree, regarding me quietly; intelligently.

Now that *really* is odd, I thought, especially because this is my dream, and that's the last thing I would have expected this brute to do. So I gathered my guts, reminded myself whose world this was, and hopped down from the tree. After I did, I ignored the tree and it disappeared, as did the hill. In a moment the entire universe was just me and the dinosaur, standing quietly together on a vast empty plain of what felt like Tupperware, under a light green sunless sky. I smiled at it. It smiled at me, and those huge sharp conical teeth seemed friendly; inviting.

"Okay," I said aloud -- perhaps, I imagined, even in the waking world, "This is totally weird."

"Not in the way you think," the great yellow beast roared, its words blowing past my face in a torrent of wind and spittle. I put up my hands in defense of the sticky stuff, but was careful not to give the impression I wanted it to go away; I was, after all, curious.

"Ho, ho!" I shouted up to its teeth, which was all I could see, "Turn it down a couple of notches there, big guy!" In response, the T-rex did something that could only be described as a shrug before it shrank in a decidedly theatrical fade from its giant monster scale down to my size. When we were eye-to-eye, I was looking at a man, of the human kind. He was about my age, with unkempt brown hair, darkish skin, and dazzling gray eyes. Oh, and he was still smiling, in a conical-toothed manner very reminiscent of my recurring dino friend.

"Sorry," he said, "Lost track of who I was there."

"And that is?"

"Huh?"

"Who is it that you are? I didn't dream you; I know that for sure."

"How do you know, for sure?"

"Because you're not yapping like a puppy."

"Oh. Okay, that's one of the better explanations I've heard."

"You didn't answer me. Who are you and what are you doing here? Unless here is somewhere you brought me; in which case you need to tell me what I'm doing there..."

His smile broke for a second when he closed his thin lips together and looked around at the scene that had not changed (unusual for me). Then those teeth -- white, straight, and not at all conical or menacing -- flashed again, and he sort of shrugged, said:

"I'm almost always 'here,' at least I have been for quite a while; waiting. Thanks for finally noticing me. And yeah, 'here' is sure enough your creation, and very much a part of you. Congrats, by the way, on the nice clean set you arranged for us."

I heard, clearly, pretty much every word he said, but it all made little sense to me. I set words aside for a second, and reached out and touched the man's cheek. It was warm, and in need of a shave. He didn't flinch, but I think his eyes might have rolled a bit at the gesture. I stepped back, folded my arms. I squinted, not sure what difference that would make. It made none. This was really weird, I thought. I've been lucid dreaming for decades, and never came across anything like this -- a dream character with his own opinions, who didn't disappear with the rest of the dream. A new line of questioning might be in order.

"Are you important?" I asked.

"Not particularly, but the folks I want to introduce you to sure are."

That forced me to pause for a moment. This had never happened to me before, and I wasn't sure how to deal with it. What I was sure of was that whatever semblance of dreaming I might have been having was behind me now, and this was something totally new. And, yes, I had a feeling it was important. So I casually scanned the empty white horizon behind the man, sighed, and said, "Okay, I'll bite. It looks like you're more than just a part of my dream, even though I don't really believe in that kind of thing, so whatever you're selling must be interesting at worst. Who are these folks?"

The man shrugged, and said, "These folks are more *what* than just who, but that doesn't matter. What does matter is that they need your help."

Uh, oh, I thought. Here it comes -- lucid or not, someone always needs my 'help.'

"So now I'm getting spammed in my dreams, too?" I asked. The man smiled broadly.

"I suppose that's exactly what this is," he said brightly, finger in the air, "And you opened the message!"

"Touché. So, what's the help?"

With that the man swirled like so much liquid back into that familiar yellow T-rex. The beast paused for a moment before it turned and walked away from me. As it walked, it said over its shoulder, "Another time, young Howard. Sadly, your nature calls and we're done for today."

I reentered the waking world seconds later, feeling indeed like I had to pee, but also, oddly, I felt very good.

Lucid Dreaming

As the reader may have surmised by now, the only practical, the only *known*, tool for communicating with the Souls is lucid dreaming. This is because the only place the prophet works is within dreams, and the only way to acknowledge his presence in your dream is by having a high level of self-awareness present when he makes his appearance. And, of course, a dream rich in self-awareness is, by definition, lucid. Only.

Though there will be discussion of lucid dreaming in this chapter, no time will be spent on the specific methods of achieving the state. As mentioned before, that is not what this book is about, and others have done an excellent job teaching the art's basics -- look to them to seek the guidance necessary to learn to properly lucid dream. You can do it on your own, but you will save much time and avoid many pitfalls simply by consulting those who have already trod this curious path.

Lucid dreaming is simply the act of bringing your "waking" self-awareness into a dream – basically being in a heightened waking state while dreaming. This may seem oxymoronic, but it can and does happen, with a frequency more widespread than people know, given that dreams are often forgotten upon waking. To be aware that you are dreaming is to open your awareness to all the stimuli inherent in dreams. Most of those stimuli are, well, unimportant, but some of it can only exist when your mind is set free during sleep to open itself.

Some of those stimuli can expose a lucid dreamer to new worlds of exploration, adventure, and enlightenment; some can even inspire transcendental experience. But, though all quite fascinating, potentially invigorating, and well worth the experience, none of that matters here. The one unique experience only a lucid dreamer can have is a conscious encounter with the avatar of the Souls – the prophet; who may have been there all along.

The lucid dreaming experience can have several levels of intensity, all of which relate directly to the quality of self-awareness a dreamer has maintained during the dream.

At the lowest level of lucidity, a dreamer realizes that the world she is currently exploring is a dream, but fails to remember that her true body is sleeping where she left it, or even that the body she occupies now is just a dream character. This level is often quite exciting, because the dreamer is consciously experiencing all the surprises and oddities of the dream, as though being swept away by it, without ever realizing that her own mind is the one doing the sweeping. The vast majority of lucid dreams are of this low-level type, or perhaps are not even lucid at all: at this level of awareness, the dreamer is still susceptible to "false lucid" dreams, wherein the dreaming mind fabricates just the right circumstances for a dream to actually be *about* being lucid, rather than actually being lucid. If a dreamer reports his dream as a long series of things happening to him, completely out of his control, there is an excellent chance that he is simply *dreaming* he is lucid, rather than actually being lucid – this is a false lucid dream. The difference between the two experiences in normal circumstances is nil, and by most measures (all of which are subjective) a false lucid dream is every bit as exciting and enlightening as a low-level actual lucid dream, and both are equally valid in terms of conscious experience. For instance, dreams of "lucidly" flying are usually false lucids, but they sure are a lot of fun! However, in our context the false lucid contains minimal validity, as there is no real chance of encountering the prophet during it. He might be present in a non-lucid dream, since by definition the dreams he attends are predominantly non-lucid, which illustrates the extreme difficulty of his task, but a more than modest level of awareness is required by the dreamer to correctly separate the prophet from the rest of the dream. Without self-awareness, a dreamer will breeze right past the prophet's avatar without note or, worse, he will errantly believe that a dream character he created is the prophet. The latter is common among those who decide to believe deeply in the prophet, but then choose to take a pass on mastering their lucid dreaming skills. The self-created prophet also tends to be more interesting to the dreamer, so it gets the most attention in the form of religions, philosophies, and paranormal scriptures. This is because the non-lucidly invented prophet will carry all the attributes the dreamer expects to find – like apparent wisdom, a long beard, maybe flowing robes – while the true prophet might have appeared in the dream as something unexpected and not so easy to accept or describe, like a bully from grade school, a squirrel, or perhaps a footstool.

The next level of lucidity carries enough self-awareness to keep the dream from controlling the dreamer, but not quite enough for the dreamer to fully control the dream. In this level, call it mediocre lucidity, the dreamer remembers who he is and where his actual body is sleeping, but cannot manage to fully accept the non-reality of the dream. When a dreamer wakes from a mediocre lucid dream, he will often describe talking to dream characters as if they were real, and talking about events in the dream as if they had actually happened. For example, his descriptions will include many phrases like, "And then this happened," or "I looked the other way and a whole new world unfolded before me, or "I listened carefully to what the old man had to say." A dreamer experiencing a mediocre lucid dream cannot change its content – even if he turns around, or flies away, he merely spurs on a new dream over which he has little control, or loses lucidity altogether. But at this level at least the dreamer cannot be fooled into believing he is lucid when he is not. Nor can he be convinced that a dream character of his own invention is the prophet. Unfortunately, at this level a dreamer is still hard-pressed to recognize the presence of the prophet. However, he might get lucky!

For instance, if the prophet manifests himself as a recurring symbol in a dreamer's world, but hasn't perfectly duplicated that symbol (as is likely), a prepared dreamer might take notice and pause to listen to him. Think of an old friend the dreamer hasn't seen for years but regularly appeared in her dreams, only this time that friend has blond hair, rather than black. Mediocre lucidity might carry enough awareness for the dreamer to notice the difference and pay attention to its oddity. That cracks the door for the prophet to speak; the opening is still but a narrow slit, but the prophet has gotten his foot into such openings in the past.

The next level could be termed "full-on" lucidity, though it would still not totally tip an awareness scale. Full-on lucidity means that the dreamer's waking awareness is fully present, self-awareness is strong, she remembers who she is and acknowledges consciously that her body in the dream is not actually hers, but that of a dream character created by her own dreaming mind. This level allows full control of the dream, including the dreamer's understanding that the dream can be abandoned for something else at any time. This level is the apex for most lucid dreamers, as it embodies the limits of conscious participation in the biological event of dreaming. At this level, the lucid dreamer would be truly remiss if she failed to spot the prophet – though the prophet says it happens often. As the lucid dreamer's awareness becomes the driver of dream events, everything in the dream, no matter how odd at its surface, becomes by definition intimately familiar to the dreamer. She recognizes that all this is hers, without exception. The trouble here is that the prophet's presence is *not* hers. Initially the dreamer will be puzzled by the avatar the prophet manifests in the dream, and she will be left with a choice: to either directly question the presence of the anathema character or symbol (remember, the prophet could appear as anything – more on that in a moment), or to assume that this oddity is simply a misplaced part of the dream, and attach her own explanation for its existence. The former is obviously the correct direction to take, but dreamers tend to choose the latter. This is because the mental and spiritual discipline necessary to both achieve a full-on lucid dream and accept that something in it is not of the dreamer's making are at odds with each other. After spending so much time and effort convincing himself that everything in a dream is of his own making, that the universe of a dream is limited to his own creation, the dreamer must now understand that his universe can be visited by the thoughts of others. This paradigm shift is not easy, and is certainly not natural. So the dreamer will often rework surprises like a visit from the prophet into his own definitions and expectations. In other words, he will attach a known metaphor to establish a context for the visiting prophet, rather than allow something completely new to enter his hard-fought creation. The pressure to define rather than welcome the prophet is difficult to surmount, but not impossible. Indeed, the exercise gets easier by simply knowing that he might be there…of course this also opens the door to "inventing" the prophet's presence when he is not there, just to satisfy long-held expectation.

This invention has an immediate negative effect on awareness, in that it reduces it: the dreamer has chosen to abandon the truth of the moment for a fiction that he can more easily fathom. Even full-on lucidity is compromised when this happens. Actually, history has shown that not only is lucidity compromised, but the dreamer tends to wake up after misidentifying the prophet. No one, including the prophet, is sure about why this happens. So basically the best bet is to be prepared to encounter the prophet during full-on lucidity with an open, attentive mind and absolute disinterest in redefining his avatar, or, worse, creating an accidental avatar on your own.

As a full-on lucid dream matures, awareness begins to eclipse lucidity, and the rules for dreaming, and the dream itself, begin to evaporate. There are levels of consciousness far higher than full-on lucid dreaming, and they are transcendent in nature. So, by definition, they simply cannot be described. Many lucid dreamers have had transcendent experiences, but failed to recognize them or remember them because, as transcendent events, no human metaphor was available for attachment to them, and the dreamer was simply unable to assimilate the event into their waking life. Transcendent events do occur frequently, the prophet insists, and they tend to be alive with communication with the Souls, with other dreamers, and blessed with spiritual encounters that span the infinite range of thought energy itself. However, none of that need be discussed here because, well, it cannot be! So back to the more mundane task of connecting with the prophet...

Because human perception, experience, and neurology have no natural basis for accommodating thought energy communication, the prophet must seek connection by laying a new foundation of essentially alien stimuli that he hopes the dreamer will perceive as something worth wrapping his awareness around. Once discovered, the prophet can work with the dreamer until a protocol for communication is established that the dreamer can easily cognate. This process can take months, even years for some, but gets progressively simpler as the dreamer grows accustomed to the language of the Souls. The most difficult period, especially for the prophet, is during the early stages, when the dreamer senses the prophet's presence but either fails to note the significance or, worse, chooses to dismiss it.

This failure is not something that should embarrass or discourage the dreamer. The prophet's first steps into a dreamer's world are tentative at best, and his initial presence is easy to misinterpret. Remember that his method for joining a dream is by assuming the shape of an object that, while familiar enough to be included in the dream, is strange enough to alert the dreamer that something needs to be investigated. Though it might make sense to a dreamer that the prophet will appear in a dream as a unique individual jumping or waving about to get attention, this almost never happens. In the early years of his odd ministry the prophet did attempt to gain attention by screaming and shouting in his human form, but the tactic failed consistently. The prophet quickly discovered that dreams are full of dream characters jumping about looking for attention; characters who often appear and sound quite deep and impressive. A dreamer, especially an advanced lucid dreamer, learns to ignore such noise and explore on her own. Now, the reader might say, "What about lucid dreamers who consult dream characters for advice? Wouldn't the prophet be quickly discovered if he assumed that role?" The prophet went that route during the 1990's heyday of lucid dreaming, sure that even the mildest lucid dreamers were being trained well enough to spot him. Unfortunately, it turns out that the only dream characters lucid dreamers consult are those that the dreamer expects to consult – all others are ignored.

Since then the prophet learned to become a specific person or object in a dream that should not have been there – a high school janitor among a choir of angels, perhaps, or a basketball perched upon a fondly remembered long-stemmed rose. Then, when the dreamer's awareness wonders about that character's/object's "wrongness," the prophet could subtly hint his presence, and the relationship would build from there. The trouble with this tactic was that even the most proficient lucid dreamer has a habit of recognizing only that which he expects to recognize, leaving oddities to be dismissed by his targeted intellect as unimportant. In other words, dreamers -- people -- tend to pay attention only to that which seems important or interesting. So dismissals became the norm. The prophet persisted. He knew that, as he had identified the Souls during his lucid dreams, lucid dreamers would in time spot him. Fortunately for the Souls, the prophet was quite patient, and in time, much time, some dreamers found him and grew to understand him.

The reader might ask if, as a novice lucid dreamer, there is any hope at all of spotting the prophet, much less conversing with him. The answer to that is simple: Yes!

If a dreamer has already built into his expectations that there might be a visit from the prophet, then half the prophet's work is complete. Any dreamer, no matter her expertise, is fully capable of perceiving the prophet. We are all wired the same, in the end. The only caveat to this is that, like the false lucids described above, expectations can lead the dreaming mind to invent its own prophet, and the true prophet goes unnoticed. Here is where attention comes into play: if you the dreamer are attentive not to what you think the prophet should be, but rather to the prophet in general, then you should eventually meet him. Be patient, be attentive, maintain a high level of self-awareness, and the prophet's presence will become apparent.

His "appearance" of course is a product of your own perception, as the prophet was likely already haunting your dreams for quite some time, unnoticed by an inattentive mind. This leads us to ask what this appearance may be. What exactly should an attentive dreamer be looking for?

That is an excellent question, whose answer one might expect to include lofty images of a god-like soul drifting nearby, open-armed. However, as mentioned above, that is simply not true -- the prophet did try that approach once, and had a 100% failure rate! It turned out that, whenever he made the effort to force an image of himself into a dream, the dreamer would interpret the image as either just another random set-piece or else he would start a new religion based on it. There was no in-between, the prophet eventually realized; either his projected god-like image was ignored or deified. Dreamers needed to attach a metaphor to define the prophet's presence, and if the image was not of their own making, correctly attaching a metaphor was impossible. Therefore, the dreamer's interpretation, during and after her dream, of the image the prophet wanted to present was always wrong. So the prophet adjusted his tactics, and now becomes an existing image in a dream so as not to be discarded or worshipped. To raise his profile with the dreamer, he makes the image he assumes stand out in a way that a lucid dreamer will notice, and then the dreamer can allow his initial image to manifest into his chosen avatar.

For example, a low-level lucid dreamer might be visiting a memory of a favorite childhood place, perhaps the toy store to which his mother often brought him when he was good. The toy store would appear to the dreamer as expected, its images drawn from established memories. Of course this store will also be stocked with the usual dreaming oddities, such as talking toys, colleagues from his waking world workplace helping him shop, aisles that seem infinite. The prophet in this case might appear as one of those toys. He does this not by inventing a new toy image, but by lending his presence to a current image. When this happens, the toy becomes something slightly different to the dreamer: perhaps that toy train he was admiring suddenly changes color, or its track might assume a Mobius-strip shape. The prophet might even borrow the shape of one of those colleagues, and say things that just do not jibe with the theme of the dream. The change would be subtle, but clear enough for an attentive lucid dreamer to notice. Once the dreamer does notice, and maintains awareness (or better yet in this case strengthens awareness, as the lucid dream is likely low-level), then the prophet will assume his preferred avatar and attempt to pass on his message.

If a dreamer has achieved full-on lucidity, the prophet's work is easier, since the dreamer has likely removed most of the dream images his own mind created, leaving a blank slate that welcomes the prophet's presence. In this case the prophet might appear as his avatar immediately or perhaps might not appear at all, but simply meld with the dreamer's awareness to initiate communication without words but with very deep meaning. Either way, the high-level lucid dreamer is prepared and open for an exchange, and is very likely to correctly infer the prophet's presence, and, should the dreamer be attentive enough, to begin to understand the message of the Souls.

Review of the last paragraphs might discourage the reader who can achieve only low-level lucidity. It should. Though low-level is better than zero awareness in a dream, it still allows too much random information to cloud perception, and that lets the image the prophet has manifest fall deeper into the background, or, worse, it gives the dreamer a chance to misinterpret his image. Low-level lucidity offers an opportunity to encounter the prophet, but it is a slim one indeed. That said, the prophet will still frequent all dreams possible, including low-level lucids, on the gamble that happy accidents do occur and a dreamer with minimal awareness might spot him, thus initiating deeper awareness and perhaps an empowering conversation.

Although the prophet may join any dream, only the highest level lucid dreamers stand a good chance of realizing that a visit is occurring, and only those with the most profound self-awareness will be able to fully profit from the encounter. But accidents do happen, even in the dream realm, so don't lose hope if you are finding it difficult to develop your lucid dreaming skills. Be prepared before going to sleep every night, build your memory skills, teach yourself to pay attention to the oddest things, and you might be able to host a visit by the prophet.

The key, as may have been mentioned before, is self-awareness and attention; develop both in waking life, and you might not only notice an object or dream character that is the prophet's avatar, but also that your lucid dreaming abilities have improved.

Brief Meditation

Below is a simple exercise which, should you master it, might help further your understanding of the Souls, thought energy and forms, the physical world, and your place among it all. Yes, this exercise potentially covers it all! Plus, it can be done during a lucid dream. If it is, then the prophet, should he be paying attention, will have an easier time connecting with you.

First, do whatever preparations best bring your mind into a proper meditative state (this author will offer no specific instructions on how to mediate – that is not what this book is about. Also, as everyone is different, and entire volumes have been written on meditation, the reader would do best to find exactly what works for him, and/or develop his own method.). Once there, replace the usual object of your focus with a very simple scene:

Picture yourself standing on or floating above a flat, perfectly smooth plain (not a plane, as we want to think more geographic than geometric in order to attain the proper mindset). This plain should be an unusual color, like purple, in order to help keep it from turning into a familiar memory or pastoral image. It should stretch to infinity in every direction. The horizon should be impossibly far off, visible only because it joins your plain to the white, perfectly empty sky.

Once you are able to conjure and hold this image for a while – be patient; an image this simple is surprisingly difficult to maintain, because of your innate need to fill a void like an empty plain with recognizable images – begin to contemplate it. Observe the plain you have created. Don't just let the plain sit there; process the metaphor from it. Decide that your plain *is* the physical universe, coursing in silent static viscosity in all directions. Then consider yourself, and notice that you are floating above the plain (aka the universe) probably without a body (if you still have a body this meditation might lack its full impact, but if you keep at it, your body will no longer be evident). You will find, in considering your self, that you are not connected to the plain. The self that is you in this meditation is not a part of the physical world, because your awareness is powered by a new source. Notice that that source, the Souls, is there above the plain with you. You may not see them, or even feel them, but remember intellectually that they are there.

When you have perfected this image, and you feel the presence of the Souls above the plain with you, then you have mastered this meditation. Of course mastery by itself is meaningless – you've merely created a metaphor with your imagination, and none of the images are real, thus they carry utterly no significance by themselves Like all meditation, it is a tool, particularly effective in helping you become aware of the nature of reality – everything is energy, period – and of the incongruence of thought energy. If the image from this meditation becomes second, um, nature to you, you may find that you can bring it into a lucid dream... then the fun begins!

First Dream Encounter: The Interview

What follows is an interview that was presented to, but never printed by, an established pop-culture magazine. Apparently one of the magazine's regular contributors was also an avid lucid dreamer who, during a high-level moment of lucidity, spotted the prophet. When this happened, the dreamer chose to encounter the prophet in a manner very familiar to him – a sit-down interview. The entire article appears below, without permission from the magazine, whose editors emphatically dismiss it as pure fiction. Its author chooses to remain anonymous, though would like to confirm that he did initially attempt to have the interview published, before waking sanity and his publisher convinced him to agree with its burial.

• • •

Many of you have heard of lucid dreaming, which is the art of maintaining your waking-life self-awareness while dreaming so that you can enjoy the adventures of your dreams while being fully aware that the experience is "only" a dream. I have been an avid practitioner of lucid dreaming for decades, and in all humility admit that I have achieved very high levels of lucidity in my dreams. While in that state I enjoyed many surprises, but the subject of this interview is by far the most fantastic (perhaps literally). Bear with me while I introduce him.

Apparently we humans have a new prophet in our midst. He comes to us as a dream avatar sent by a remarkable group of beings he calls the Seven Souls. This prophet (as he himself suggested I describe him, reluctantly, I think) has for the last several years been appearing in the dreams of virtually everybody, regardless of race, color, creed, or nationality. This ethereal visitor is almost never noticed by dreamers of "normal" dreams, but somehow lucid dreaming provides just enough awareness for a dreamer to spot him. That spotting is difficult at best, and serendipitous in the norm, because the prophet can only appear in dreams as something the dreamer invented. That invention can be anything from a familiar relative to a small rock teetering on a distant wall. Once he is noticed, however, the prophet invites conversation, even as a rock, and in that conversation relates a remarkable story that, if true, hints at great things to come for the dreamer, and ultimately all of humanity.

I will withhold the specific sordid details of my dream, but suffice it to say that during an advanced lucid dream I noticed at the very limit of my peripheral vision an object that seemed not to belong there. I looked directly at it. Initially it seemed to be an oddly colored version of a mailbox, but when I held my attention on it for a few seconds, it morphed into a young man, perhaps in his early thirties, of medium build and height and indeterminate ethnicity (I was sure the fellow's skin tone and hair color kept shifting, but something wouldn't allow me to focus on the changes). He wore old jeans, a red t-shirt sans logo, and no shoes. I had been studying dreams for many years, and knew to look for the "odd" in life and dreams to best gain awareness that I was dreaming. Well this guy was odd, so I knew, and thus began my interview with the Dream Prophet:

Lucid Dreamer: You're not supposed to be here, are you?

Dream Prophet (looking completely nonplused as he settled his jeans & t-shirted self into a settee that appeared a few feet from the wingback chair I now occupied): That's up to you, I suppose. Where's here?

LD: In my dream, I think.

DP: Then yes, since you've spotted me, I probably should be here.

LD: Why?

DP: We're doing an interview, aren't we?

LD: So you know who I am.

DP: Of course. It's your dream, after all! As a guest in your world, I know you as well as your mind can define you.

LD: That's startling.

DP: Not really. In fact, you'd be amazed at how many minds I've visited whose dreams left me totally in the dark.

LD: That's not a shock, I suppose. So then is it okay if I ask a few questions?

DP: S'why I'm here.

LD: Well, first the obvious: who are you? And please don't say you're me.

DP: Okay I won't. But I'm not doing so because I'm a nice guy -- which I am. I'm not saying I'm you because, frankly, I'm not. This is not your father's psychology class; it's the real world, where things not of your creation can exist. Not only am I not something you dreamed up, I'm really very different from you. But I *should* be here, because we share a similar mission...

LD: Okay, hold that thought. If I remember I'll go back to it. First, though: who are you?

DP: Does that matter?

LD: It will to my readers...should I still have any if I manage the two impossible tasks of remembering all this and convincing my magazine to print it.

DP: You'll manage at least half that, I'd bet. Anyway; who I am is not really important, but you can call me prophet. Or the prophet, I guess -- I never know which to use, and honestly neither thrills me.

LD: Okay. Though that's a fairly weighty moniker, it really tells me nothing I want to hear. I was hoping for a name.

DP: Sorry. ID's only manage to confuse on this plane. Tell you what: you can call me Bob, if you'd like.

LD: Okay Prophet Bob, we'll set "who" aside for now. Where are you from?

DP: Whew, I thought you were going to ask me *what* I was next.

LD: That's coming…

DP: Figured. Anyway, I'm from Ramapo, New Jersey, originally.

LD: So, Ramapo New Jersey has a door into people's dreams? Did you buy it at IKEA?

DP (laughs): I said originally – I started out there, a very long time ago. I'm not from anywhere in particular anymore.

LD: Are you still among the living?

DP: Do you talk to dead people?

LD: None that I know of. Do you?

DP: There are no dead people.

LD (after a long pensive pause): Is that supposed to be deep? Or scary?

DP: Nope.

LD: Well, it is, so I'll ignore it until, or perhaps should, my nerve hardens. Next here's a shallow softball question: is that what you really look like?

DP: You ask me that, yet in your last few minutes of experiencing me I've been tall, short, blond, bald, and even female for a second. Which of those should I say is what I look like?

LD: (After a pause to realize that the prophet wasn't kidding) Whoa. You're right. So what you're telling me is that you take shape at the dreamer's whim?

DP: Yup; and you've got a lot of whim.

LD: Ha Ha. What's the most unusual form you've been given by us dreamers?

DP: Well, I was a doorstop once. That was a bizarre experience on many levels.

LD: So tell me, Prophet Bob, if we could come back full circle. Why are you here?

DP: I guess because you noticed me.

LD: Does that mean you're always here? In my dreams?

DP: Uh huh. And don't get cocky; I try my best to dip my toe in everyone's dreams.

LD: Seriously? All seven billion of us?

DP: Closer to six, really -- it's amazing how poorly the 'experts' measure things. And I suppose that number is really three, since about half the world is awake and generally not dreaming at any given time. But yeah, seriously; I endeavor to maintain a presence in the dreams of all humanity. One at a time, and all at once.

LD: That sounds like a lot of work. But I guess if Santa can do it once a year...

DP: Yeah, and he has to deliver toys, too. I just have thoughts, and they are way easier to keep in the sleigh.

LD: So what about that similar mission we share?

DP: You remembered!

LD: That is what I do. You're shaking your head, though: is it not yet time to ask about that mission?

DP: Nope.

LD: Why?

DP: First you have to ask who sent me, and who want to recruit you for this mission.

LD: Oh. Sorry. So, um, who sent you?

DP: Nobody really – I came on my own. But I do have a message from mutual friends.

LD: Mutual friends? Who?

DP: (suddenly rubbing his temples) Um, maybe I got ahead of myself here. Let's hold off on the deep shit for now…or for good. That's not what this first contact is about.

LD: First contact. What? Are your friends aliens?

DP: I get that a lot; I really should find new terms. No. My friends are not aliens. They are from right here as much as we are. In a sense I suppose they *are* us, more than you could imagine. But at the same time they are so different from us they cannot even communicate directly with us (even though they exist all around us).

LD: You're speaking in circles, Prophet Bob. Tell me, who are our friends?

DP: They like to be called Souls. There are seven of them.

LD: What are they? I'm pretty sure I know what a soul is (that drew a smile from the prophet)…

DP: Of course you do. Even so, here's what they are, in a rough nutshell: the Souls are seven eternal beings comprised of a physics-defying sort of coherent thought energy who were enjoying eternal perfection in a world without space, time, or anything we call real, when their essence was violently torn apart and thrust into every atom of this universe when it was created by an eighth Soul (who died in the process). Though they were still fairly cohesive entities when the universe was young, its expansion has not been good for them: they've been spread pretty thinly over the last 15 billion years.

LD: I thought it was 13 billion years.

DP: Fifteen. Trust me. I hope you heard the rest of the description. Anyway, the Souls have been waiting all those years for a group of sentient beings to emerge armed with enough self-awareness, intellectual wherewithal, imagination, and interest to form the thought energy necessary to return the Souls to their original perfect state.

LD: Huh?

DP: You asked. That's the best I can do in this meeting. I know it makes little sense like this, but fully explaining it all to you could take years.

LD: Okay, that's humbling. But I'll bite. Is there anything you want me, or humanity in general (since I might be sharing this conversation with them) to do while we wait to learn about these Souls, and their charge?

DP: Amazing how you writer types can actually pronounce the upper case. The Souls do have a sincere suggestion, actually.

LD: Okay, what's that?

DP (leaning forward conspiratorially, and then whispering, after a pause of at least ten beats): Be nice to each other.

LD: That's it?

DP: That's really a lot, if you think about it, and the Souls are depending on it; on us. Since the dawn of all sentience, that is the only thing that matters. We need to be nice to each other in order for thought energy to be formed properly: good thoughts produce thought energy that's amenable to helping the Souls' ultimate reconstitution. Plus, bad thoughts build bad souls, and apparently each of us is constructing a soul of our own with every thought we produce. So the condition of our own eternal being is dependent on the quality of our thoughts. I know, I know: none of this makes much sense. Since you'll be waking up shortly, suffice it to say that, for the first time in earth's history, there are signs that the whole being nice to each other thing has potential to actually happen. Haven't you noticed any changes lately?

LD: In all honesty, no. The world seems knee-deep in the same sticky swamp of meanness that has always mired it. Technology might have changed, but we're all still the same.

DP: Are we? Think about it, very hard, after you wake up. You might be surprised. Humanity is poised for change, for spiritual improvement, like it has never been poised before. We are ready to finally get along with each other on a personal and global scale, and that is the attitude necessary for the Souls' success.

LD: Spiritual improvement? That sounds very religious. Are we talking religion, here?

DP: Absolutely not. In fact, the major human religions are a reflection of the Souls' failed past attempts to get their message across. Before we were ready, people, including my predecessors, had an accidental knack for turning the Souls' mission into a man-made religion. For example, think of what Jesus really said during his ministry; it could all be pared down to "be nice to each other – the other stuff doesn't matter." Then look what his message got turned into. We weren't ready, then. We might be, now.

LD: Did you just compare yourself to Jesus Christ?

DP (sighing): That's all you heard, again? No matter. No, I don't compare myself to Mr. Christ. Not directly. But you see how the "other stuff" lingers, even in your own psyche? You heard me make that comparison, even though I really did not. And had I taken up Christ's mantle vocally, you would have immediately questioned my sanity.

LD: But I didn't. And I'm pretty sure I ultimately wouldn't, regardless of the initial knee-jerk intellectual crap that my mouth might eject out of habit.

DP: See? We *are* growing up.

LD: Okay. Anyway, since there won't be more chat about the big stuff, then back to you. Your personal mission is to dip into people's minds and tell them what to do?

DP (head shaking): No, on both counts. I am in their dreams, yes. But I don't do any "mind dipping." It's the exact opposite: I wait at the outskirts of a dream, fundamentally unobtrusive, until the dreamer is both able to and cares to pay enough attention to draw my presence into their conscious experience. I will never tell anyone what to do – that won't work with humans, especially the ones who just spent years working on their own initiative to lucid dream.

No, given time I will teach them to communicate directly with the Souls, who also will only ask, never demand.

LD: And still you won't share exactly what the Souls are, what this thought energy is, and exactly why humans are so damn critical to whatever those answers are?

DP: Nope. Not today. There just isn't time.

LD: And I'm supposed to graciously accept these noncommittal, arguably empty proclamations at face value?

DP: Yup. And that's without me even having given you their face value.

LD: Why on earth would I do that?

DP: You've already done it. Let's consider the veracity part: this is your dream, your spiritual world. Why would I bother holding anything back, since, given you have the final judgment in your realm, you will either dismiss or forget our encounter in the morning? If you're not buying any of this, my story and I will be long gone from your personal universe before your first cup of coffee. Even if you're on board, you're still effectively alone: try sharing those truths in waking life without risking being put away! In other words, if you remember, or worse dare to retell my 'empty' proclamations, it means you've already decided both to make them important enough to remember, and risk sharing them with your cynical neighbors. Finally, since the only way anyone other than you can know about my words to you is through your writing them down, then, yes, in terms of your readers' cognition, you have already done it.

LD: Excellent point, and food for thought over that coffee in a few hours.

DP: Minutes, by my watch.

LD: Dream ghosts have watches?

DP: Of course not; time doesn't even exist outside physical sentient experience, much less timepieces. I was waxing metaphoric.

LD: Wow, deep. Okay, now how about this...

DP: Nope. I hate to say it, but your alarm is about to go off.

LD: You mean metaphorically, of course.

DP: Uh uh. For real.

LD: That will work?

DP: Of course; you're just asleep, after all. This ain't no magical mystical tour you're on.

LD: Had to make a musical reference, didn't you?

DP: Thought it might impress your editors -- they do still report on musical stuff right? Maybe it'll help you get this published. No matter, though -- it is time to wake up.

LD: But this was fun, and there was so much more to ask, I'm sure. I never even got to ask what you are. It can't end now.

DP: Oh yes it can. Nice memory work, though; that is important.

LD: What if I choose not to wake up?

DP: Not your choice. You know that.

LD: Damn; I do. Will you be back?

DP: That's up to you, and your ability to pay attention.

The Charge

Much has been discussed about the Souls, their history, their prophet, and even what they stand to gain from human participation in their work. However, you may still be wondering: why am I reading this? What about the humans? What do we get from this transaction? Or, less selfishly, what is our contribution to this transaction, and how will it help?

The answers to those questions are both simple and also quite complex. First and foremost, what we "get" from this transaction is by definition impossible to describe, since the greatest gift the Souls have to offer is a real chance to experience, to literally share, their spiritual existence. This alone should be enough, as it represents what could be the next step in human evolution – one of transcendent consciousness, of mind. But, since it is beyond understanding until (and often after) it is experienced, any words describing it are nothing more than pure conjecture that cannot hope to touch the reality of the experience. Because of that, I will pass right over the complex and glorious part, leaving it to the readers' imaginations, since in its case their opinion is every bit as valid as mine.

The simple end is that we have an opportunity to learn how to better understand ourselves, our universe, and our place in it. Just the experience of successfully meeting the prophet in a dream, and perhaps even an introduction to the Souls, is enough to prove that there is indeed "something" out there -- something that exceeds our very short span of physical existence on this little planet, and our very limited personal perceptions of reality. Beyond that, there is also the practical addition to our lives that understanding and using thought energy would provide. Though manipulating thought energy would be an art learned by very few over much time, and carries a potential (though very unlikely) threat to physical reality itself, it is certainly a tangible reward for working with the Souls.

On a higher level, the Souls could prove a unifying factor for all peoples. As more individuals become aware of them, of themselves, and of the powerful untapped resource that is thought energy, the cultural scourges of religious and ethnic competition, material wealth, jealousy, narcissism, and hate might at last begin to lose their fabricated priority. The damage they do to our world and our own spiritual futures might finally become a readily discarded memory.

That said, the Souls have no material requirements, and ask for nothing from us save developing and coordinating organized thought energy capable of returning them to their primordial existence. The prophet, however, has said that the Souls have indeed listed one charge, one commandment, as it were, that they insist will make the process of their reconstitution go more smoothly: be nice to each other.

The Souls are well aware that an act of blind selfishness destroyed their universe (albeit creating ours in the process), and they know that the same disregard for fellow beings could unravel our own destiny, while prolonging their cosmic entrapment, if humanity continues on a path strewn with the debris of people, and peoples, who choose to not be nice to each other.

The Souls have endeavored to convince sentients to do this simple yet genetically difficult thing since time began with, as noted earlier, limited results every time. Their attempts with humans came closest to success with Jesus of Nazareth two millennia ago. Typically, though Jesus, who understood his mission, sought no more than to be avatar for the Souls and show his people a new way of being, his work was mangled by a marked lack of self-awareness in his followers. Even though his sermons, parables, and, yes, travels into the dreams of his contemporaries' minds (as averred by the prophet), were universally anti-religion, the nature of the cultures he navigated caused his message to be beaten over time into a religion. Because it carried a powerful message, and Jesus really did struggle to convey it, his work was not only translated into a religion, but into an immortal one, overseen by complex church systems run by limited-sighted people whose worldly agenda often dismissed or overlooked Jesus' Golden Rule. As the centuries passed and Jesus' visit grew distant with time, being nice, especially to people who are not the same as you, has been all but forgotten. It might be mentioned here that Jesus' ministry was not confined to his immediate vicinity: he was able to touch the dreams of peoples worldwide, having the greatest success with the eastern cultures. This was most notable among the Buddhists who, while still applying religious import to his visits, did manage to hold onto both the "be nice" theme and the significance of the Souls (if not their actual existence and need).

The Souls believe that the 'givens' for modern humanity bode well for them: the sudden 20th century growth spurt in technology, philosophic absorption of $e=mc^2$ and its metaphysic children into most societies, the near groupmind nature of the internet, and an unprecedented worldwide trend toward disinterest in war, all imply that humanity may be ready to pay more correct attention to this particular prophet. The Souls are confident that this time, if the prophet is successful in gathering willing minds to their cause, that those minds will have the mental maturity to be careful to avoid turning the Souls' cause into a new religion. They know that would be a very bad thing, in that thought energy cannot be formed in novel ways when thoughts are constrained by the dogma of invented worship. The Souls hope that the lessons of the errors of the major religions will be enough to convince newly self-aware people to focus on simply being nice, and resist the urge to formalize their work or, worse, rationalize it into something that it is absolutely not.

The prophet, being human, has his doubts about this, and is working hard to convince his listeners not to consider or promote some new mythology, or how the Souls are just like God, etc. He knows where those thoughts lead, especially among weaker minds in need of a handy deep-sounding metaphysical hangar from which to cling. But he knows that the basis of the Souls' charge -- to be nice to each other -- is indeed critical to their, and our future, so he does include it in his messages. He hopes that, as more dreamers find him and understand him, there will be a natural flow towards a posture of being nice among at least all of those dreamers, and that they might not look beyond that simple rule 'for more,' simply because what they are experiencing during their encounters with the Souls is enough in itself. This flow, he hopes, will become epidemic, and being nice should become a cornerstone of self-awareness upon which the Souls can build a thought energy bridge toward both their redemption and our spiritual evolution.

What about love, you might ask, given that so much of human existence is dedicated to it? Why isn't there a charge to love one another? Well, it's a funny thing -- the Souls originally knew nothing of love, as it is an emotion encoded in the physical universe meant to further reproduction. The Souls were certainly told about love, as long ago as the Raptors' time, but never placed much value in it. That humans have made love so important in their lives and general mythos is wonderful, they concede, but that elevation has no real value, save to complicate human lives, now that reproduction is no longer their primary driver for personal existence. In a sense, love really has nothing to do with the Souls, thought energy, or their salvation, so they take a pass in even trying to understand our metaphysical obsession with it.

And of course, the Prophet dangles that other carrot before us, one that the Souls themselves have overlooked as obvious. Being nice has another, far more intimate long-term result: our own personal souls, that pool of energy we are accumulating over our lifetimes, that waits to be energized by our conscious input after the death of our physical bodies, will be far more vigorous when fueled by a lifetime of good thoughts.

First Dream Encounter: Gloria

Sometimes, no, very often, waking life just gets to be too much for me, and I need more than anything else to get away; away from the people at the store where I work, away from my family, away from "friends" who care little for me beyond my presence for their complaints, away from the bills, the traffic, and everything else…you know the drill. My friend Alice told me about lucid dreaming, and saved my life. Literally. So now, when it's all too much, I just plug my awareness into my sleeping world and go to the dream scene that follows for a little peace and solitude. It almost always works, and when it does it's always the same -- peaceful. Once, though, things did not go as planned:

As is my habit, I drifted from waking life straight into my dream (they tell me this is a WILD, for "Wake Induced Lucid Dream," which I think is pretty cool), and was immediately lounging in my little yellow rubber raft, wearing that little black dress that feels so good against my skin. I was floating but motionless, adrift in an endless sea of glass-smooth black water under a soft sunless gray sky. The silence and solitude were absolute. Everything was perfect. Until I heard that bell.

It was ringing behind me, with a steady dull clang that sounded way too much like a death-knell. I tried to ignore it, but it kept sounding its bong, bong, bong, ever so slowly. I tried to just make it go away, which I should have been able to do easily, but the slow tolling continued. I swung one leg over the side of my raft and dipped my bare foot into the cool water. I gave a little kick to turn the raft around. It spun slowly, and for a moment I was at peace again (between bongs) as I scanned the empty horizon that passed without change as the raft spun around -- I wouldn't even have noticed the movement, if that red buoy hadn't suddenly broken the horizon by appearing from off to my left. It then drifted slowly into the center of my vision, rudely splitting my perfect world in two. Once it was dead ahead of me, my raft stopped turning.

The buoy drifted a few hundred yards off my little rubber bow. It was one of those old bell buoys that would bob in the waves to warn sailors of impending doom (usually rocks -- I hate rocks). The bobbing made the bell work. This buoy was, as my invented universe demanded, stock still on the placid water. Yet it continued its slow bong, bong, bonging. And it was drifting closer, on the current-free surface.

"Go away!" I shouted, flexing my wet foot slightly to kick up a great wall of water that inundated the buoy. It didn't even lean over, and the cadence of the bongs went unchanged. This is all wrong. I thought. With that thought, the tolling stopped. Hmm, I thought, maybe it's not so wrong; just different. Then the buoy sounded once, in a much less death-tollie voice this time. I felt my dream-character mouth crinkle up in a smile. I was getting it, finally: this buoy wasn't mine. It came from somewhere else, and was trying to get me to listen to its now gentle dings.

Well, I thought, I would be a bit of a hypocrite to ignore it, so:

"What?" I shouted at it, my voice accidentally booming god-loud across the water. The dinging stopped. I waited, patiently at first, as the buoy sat there in silence. I hoped I hadn't hurt its big metal feelings with my shout, but it was spilt milk at that point. Then, concerned that I might be waking up soon and time was short, I decided to take the initiative and blew a puff of air at the front wall of my raft. It obediently moved toward the buoy, which was right beside me instantly. It was much smaller and cleaner than I thought it would be. And it looked soft. I touched it.

What came next is difficult to explain, because you really had to be there, but I'll try. When I touched the buoy, it changed. Everything changed. Okay, it didn't really change -- it was still a red warning buoy floating by my little rubber raft. The water was gone, so I suppose something changed. Now we floated on nothing; at least either I remember it was nothing, or else it might as well have been nothing, because I just didn't care about the backdrop anymore. Only the buoy.

So I touched it. And when I did it spoke to me. It didn't talk with words, or more of those damn bongs, but instead it spoke through that touch. I knew, just by laying my dream-character-me's fingers gently on that oddly soft red surface, exactly why that buoy had invaded my dream, and that what it wanted was a truly good thing. I tried to speak to it, or maybe him, I guessed, as there was definitely a soul buried under that gentle surface:

"Who are you?" I asked. The buoy answered by vibrating ever so gently. Within the vibration I could feel his intent, his kindness, and, above all, absolute confirmation that there is something more than just me, this skinny unwanted body, and this ugly ugly world I try so hard not to hate every day.

I think we 'spoke' some more, but I honestly either can't remember, or else just as honestly can't figure out how to translate what we said into words. It was real, though, and for the first time in my life I woke up with hope in my heart, and purpose on my mind.

I have since been refining my skills, and am sure that I have met, in many forms, some actually human, the man inside that buoy. Almost everything that has happened after each meeting started is either completely forgotten, intentionally not remembered, or just never happened -- I don't know. What I do know is that I always feel very good when I go to sleep, even better when I wake up, and I haven't needed that glass-smooth sea in a very, very long time.

The Future

$\mathbf{A}$ curious, unprecedented event is likely to befall humanity within the next century. This event will change humanity like nothing has before. When it happens, suddenly from an historic standpoint, much of humanity will be left in turmoil, or simply left behind while the prepared few ride the wave of this change to new heights, new adventures, and perhaps a new way of being human. One of the ways to join the prepared few is by working with the Souls, paying attention to them, and learning from them. There are certainly other preparations to be made for this event, but they do not need to be discussed here.

What is this event? Call it a confluence of technology, philosophy, sociology, ecology, and likely a bunch of other ologies as they each revise the limits of knowledge and achievement in a way that will impact, possibly even decimate life as we know it – and that will be a good thing, for those who are prepared.

Rather than offer long explanations couched in arguable theory, hazy long range predictions, and interpretations of history that will do little to maintain the theme of this book, let me instead offer a list to consider (in no particular order of importance):

- Global Warming
- Universally available Internet/World   Wide Web
- The Large Hadron Collider
- Medical breakthroughs including the eradication of most disease, cancers, and an end to aging as we know it.
- Successful genetic manipulation and cloning.
- Nanotechnology
- The end of oil.
- Global population decline
- Quantum computing
- Continued deployment of advanced space-based telescopes.

There will of course be more world-changing discoveries that still lie beyond our consideration – who knows what paradigm shifts the human imagination will install in the next generation or two? The point is that the items on this list will present more advancements in human technology alone than have been made in the entire history of the human race – including fire and agriculture. Nanotechnology promises (threatens?) to change everything we know, and also eliminate the need for individual humans to do anything at all, workwise, and still not only survive but thrive physically. That we can abandon every instinct and live just to live is both staggeringly exciting and, to a very large chunk of the population, paralyzingly terrifying. If the promises of nanotechnology are combined with almost unavoidable advances in medicine, and they will be, we will have a universally long-lived population with nothing to do, in terms of working to survive. In fact, there is a chance that many, many people will spiritually digress as their physical needs are accounted for without any real personal input -- individuals often define themselves by their ability to survive and maintain comfort and security; removal of those things from their life's equation may make them feel empty indeed. Dealing with this will be most challenging for the human population as a whole, and the Souls have seen entire civilizations decay for lack of purpose (the cetaceans being a profound example). However, adaptation is not impossible, and will come easily to those who have high self-awareness and have already seen the possibilities the Souls present. After all, if a person is already in direct communication with eternal beings who can generate, perceive, and understand universally-instant thought energy, then the history-busting changes of that list would seem to her like baby steps indeed!

The one major aspect of nanotechnology that continues to vex engineers is interface. Sure, we can build machines, computers, and whatever else on an atomic scale, but how do we talk to them? Perhaps thought energy, and specifically directed thought forms, is the answer to that problem. The Souls have hinted that it is, and, when we've developed nanotechnology to the point where interface is needed, they have also hinted that they are willing to help us create that interface. Again, they seem willing to do this even if we do not choose to attend to their wish to return to their original existence; they likely sense that our adaptation of thought energy into our technology (and our reality) will only help to eventually bring us to them. They are quite patient.

And that is just nanotechnology. Entire books can and will be written about the potential and then realized impact of any and all of the rest of the items on the list above. The fantastic changes to reality itself that quantum computers alone will likely cause are mind-boggling on their own. Mix that with the devastating effects and accompanying geopolitical desperation of global warming and the last extracted drops of oil, the existential shock of the physics community when the LHC fails to discover a Higgs particle, the wholesale change in the world aristocracy's value of life when it learns that cloning is available to them, the fact that anyone will live to 150, people worldwide are having fewer kids, and that everyone – *everyone* – knows exactly what is going on thanks to the internet, and you have a paradigm soup like none brewed by any other era in our history. And these predictions are based on what we know about today. What happens when we learn new things tomorrow? A huge wave of change is rising on humanity's distant horizon. Currently, its impact will be survived only by the very rich, the scientifically connected, and those who can otherwise ride the crest of the wave of change that is guaranteed to inundate every aspect of what humanity currently considers unchangeable reality.

Today, there is no practical way to safely navigate the crest of that wave, unless you indeed are extremely rich or extremely tied in with the scientific community. Extremely lucky will not help, so don't bother to hold out hope for that. As in the past, praying for salvation won't help either. Like it or not, a vast chunk of the human population will be trampled by the changes instilled by the confluence of events like the ones listed above. That said, we who are not rich or well connected are not all doomed...

The prophet has mentioned the coming conflagration to as many dreamers who would listen, and he mentions it not with an air of doom, but with one of real hope. He cites a two-pronged solution offered by the Souls: first, if being nice to each other becomes a truly universal movement, then the bulk of humanity will find compassionate, self-aware hands reaching down to them from the crest of that wave. Those compassionate fingers will be limited in their grasp, however, as only the reasonably self-aware among us will even know that they are there, and only the spiritually strong among us will have the sense and humility to spot, reach for, and hold fast to those extended hands. That is because being nice to each other works, without exception, in both directions, just as it tends to fail when only cast one way. Second, the Prophet assures us that those with powerful self-awareness will likely find a way to surf to the crest of that wave before it breaks upon history itself. That 'way' will include lucid dreaming, contact with the prophet and perhaps the Souls, and, above all else, absolute knowledge that, whatever happens in this particular physical world, there truly is a potential eternity of joyful growth and exploration via a thought energy-charged soul assembled from a lifetime of good thoughts, and a single second of self-awareness at the point of physical death. With that hand in play, whatever the changes the physical world holds will seem inconsequential indeed!

Also by Peter A. Luber:

Works of Fiction:

Oneironauticus

ISBN: 978-0-6151-8290-2

Party Line

ISBN: 978-0-578-03593-2

Published by Sageous

CPSIA information can be obtained at www.ICGtesting.com
234645LV00001B/71/P

9 780615 454177